WORK FROM HOME
HOME

JOBS For Moms

Passive Income Ideas
for financial freedom life
with your Family

12 REAL SMALL BUSINESSES YOU CAN
DO RIGHT NOW

By
Rebecca Rightime

Mira Star Publisher web site:

www.mirastarpublisher.com

Disclaimer

The content of this book has been checked and compiled with great care. For the completeness, correctness and topicality of the contents however no guarantee or guarantee can be taken over. The content of this book represents the personal experience and opinion of the author and is for entertainment purposes only. The content should not be confused with medical help.

There will be no legal responsibility or liability for damages resulting from counterproductive exercise or errors by the reader. No guarantee can be given for success. The author therefore assumes no responsibility for the non-achievement of the goals described in the book.

Do you want to enjoy your life with your family, spend more time with them, and take more care of them without worrying about money all the time?

Do you wish to have a passive income source so that you can focus on your family life more instead of working 9 to 5 for earning money?

Does investing seem confusing to you?

If so, then keep reading!

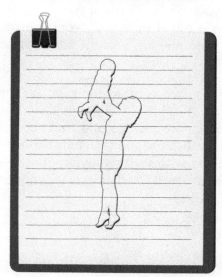

There are two types of income sources. One is active and another one is passive. Active income is when you are working and you are getting paid for the amount of work you have done. Passive income is the type of income that comes rolling in without putting effort. In passive income, you will be earning even when you are spending time with your children and even when you are on a family picnic. People become rich and enjoy their lives with passive income sources.

Passive income might seem a little confusing to you but it does not have to be overwhelming or confusing once you read this book. We have provided you with step by step guideline in details which are easy to understand and follow. It will be an amazing experience for you to watch your investments grow and reach your goals. The best part is that you will be able to spend much time with your family members and kids while making a profit and retire early with excitement.

Be financially free completely with our outstretched and manifested guide. It will provide you with skill, knowledge, and secret tips and tricks to turn around your financial life for good. Handle family better and have more fun with them watching money streaming to you without effort. And all this without enrolling in expensive classes

Here's what makes this book special:

- Secret tips and tricks to manage your finances properly;
- Find the path to financial freedom and learn the key to wealth creation;
- Make easy money effortlessly entering the world of passive income;
- Learn 12 businesses ideas as a mom while staying more with your family at home;
- Earn through Kindle publishing;
- Build niche websites to sale your interests;
- Sell online courses on udemy.;
- Learn affiliate marketing, making landing pages, email lists and many more;

Know the in and out of passive income. Unlock the profit-making potential you have inside you with this guide and follow the path that the rich people have always followed. Passive income is the only key to become rich and enjoy life at the same time. With our guide, learn all the work from home ideas and master the game of passive income for a financial freedom life insurance. Walk away from boring 9 to 5 jobs, earn passive income and retire early.

So, interested in financial freedom in the 21st century?

Then, just keep reading...

Table of contents

INTRODUCTION

- **Do you dream about achieving true financial freedom?**
- **Do you want more time to spend with your family and friends or do the things you love?**

All through this book, you will discover extra about what cash autonomy can be and figure out how it might affect you in unequivocal. A big part of changing into monetarily free is breaking new ground and thinking beyond practical boundaries. This book urges you to discover those fantasies and fabricate them with essential objectives to begin working toward. With each 50% of the book, you will start to interface your gigantic dreams to concrete goals that can type the possibility of your excursion to cash autonomy. Each progression can, in flip, offer the necessary structure impedes that will give you the reasonable devices you need to understand those fantasies. In the essential portion of this book, you may discover more about some fundamental abilities and practices that will return helpful as you're utilized through the things to do. These are quite essential advances fixated on your goals and the clarifications for beginning this excursion.

Expect how you have returned to smoking a few times or quit heading out to the rec center as regularly as you might want. I need to make right this won't occur to you on your excursion to cash autonomy, regardless of whether you feel your inspiration plunging every so often. In this manner, the underlying and conjointly most significant advance on your excursion is to make a genuine obligation to your central goal.

• You may feel you have just dedicated by picking up this book or because you have been agonizing about understanding your funds for an incredibly lengthy timespan that you sense your psyche is prepared for the test. Notwithstanding, sooner or later, you will be more likely than not to lose the will to proceed with some underlying obstacles.

• Consequently, help yourself out and focus on the 100 stages to financial autonomy here these days. At present, your desire is at its most elevated. (Remember those people with New Year's goals. They also were once basically, however, persuaded as you may be as of now.) The financial opportunity could be a phase at which you can experience your fantasies that are a long way past your present way of life. It implies you'll do regardless of what you need to attempt to. However,(monetarily) and that money is no worry.

• Your purpose behind starting this excursion might be to have the option to purchase various vehicles, live a large portion of the year in your second house inside the Caribbean, and blessing everybody in your family with the latest gadget. Or, on the other hand, you may wish to take it another way and offer away generous segments of your abundance to noble cause or established your foundation, become an altruist, or encourage salvage our planet.

Outrageous as this motivation to seek after money-related autonomy would be perhaps trustworthy; numerous people accomplish this objective, subsequently who knows whether you may moreover, with time? 65, and in this book, I'll show you the means you wish to need to design your way to exiting the workforce.

Having the money to resign early recommends that you will not need to go to work you're 65 or maybe more established to begin carrying on with your everyday routine the strategy you wish to experience. At the point when you have the money to resign at fifty, forty, or even thirty years old, your point of view will be unique. You will want to quit working on another person's terms lastly carries on with life the methods you need to. People who have prevailed at resigning early form their choices about existence dependent on what looks right to them rather than what every other person is doing.

They settle on decisions that license them the opportunity; this suggests they are intensely mindful of each money related call they have and its effect on their retirement plans. Various people have shocking thoughts concerning what it proposes that to resign early. For a few, exiting the workforce suggests that having the option to leave at age sixty. For other people, their withdrawal from the workforce dream intends to have the opportunity to resign at age 35. As per the Social Security Administration, full retirement age (FRA) is between age sixty-5 and 67, depending on the year you were conceived. This can be the point at which you'll begin gathering full Social Security edges. On the off chance that you select to resign and start drawing on your Social Security benefits before your FRA, you might be punished with more modest advantage checks. Nonetheless, by keeping the guidelines during this book, you'll have the option to resign as ahead of schedule as you might want without requiring Social Security benefits.

As I examine the best approach to form your withdrawal from the workforce plan (ERP), I will help you plan as though you're not visiting get Social Security retirement favorable circumstances. In this strategy, any Social Security retirement edges you get later on will be an expansion to your pay instead of something you'll rely upon. Despite what your objective exit from the workforce age is, there are different edges to having the monetary proposes that to have the option to resign early. Individuals who can leave before having the freedom to travel, to invest energy with family, to commit themselves to leisure activities, to start their own business, or perhaps to head out back to secondary school. At the point when you've arranged your accounts in a revolutionary approach that allows you to have the option to leave your place of employment, you'll invest some energy doing things you need to attempt to secondary school and quit being stuck during a task that gives you nothing a great deal of than a fortnightly check.

What does exit the workforce indeed appear as? The appropriate response differs from individual to individual. However, most concur that they need to resign ahead of schedule to permit them to attempt to do the things they wish to try to secondary school. In all honesty, making a set up for exiting the workforce is a great deal of not so messy. All you might want is sufficient pay to produce resources for your everyday costs for the rest of your life. Right now, we should see how to accomplish that objective.

Chapter 1

Planning to Spend more Time with Your Family? Tips to Manage Your Finances

With the economy in decline, thinking about being able to retire to finally have time to be with your family members may seem extravagant.

Notwithstanding, if you are included in your retirement years' cash security, you must not be kidding concerning monetary retirement arranging. Cash retirement concocting is the initial step to guarantee that the way to deal with life you're longing for at retirement can have a superior possibility of turning into a reality. Regardless of how past or youthful you're, it's never the inaccurate chance to consider money related retirement thinking and start a retirement investment funds mastermind. Nonetheless, the sooner you get, the better going you'll be. The odds are you will have more significant savings at retirement if you begin saving at 30 years of age instead of sixty. With extra years to hypothesize, your venture can have a superior possibility of recuperating from any drops or knock along the methods.

The more extended your money is contributed, the higher your likelihood of getting your future. By planning for your retirement wants, you will distinguish what you need to do to get your lot and be in an exceptionally higher situation to oblige most issues that may some way or another befuddle you and do damage to you monetarily. The essential idea for your retirement reserve funds orchestrates can be the place where your venture cash will go and for a way long. As a critical technique, you should put a portion of your money in a nutshell, term speculation, medium-term ventures, and long-haul ventures. Your time skyline chooses such an experience as a rule. For the most part, a ton of time you have before emptying the experience for cash, the less secure the speculation. On the off chance that your time skyline is at least five years, which would be considered long haul ventures, you'll have the option to pick speculations that increase in value after some time. Development stocks and realty are reasonable long-haul ventures if you have numerous years left before retirement.

Unpredictable stocks or CDs are considered transient ventures, speculations held for a year or less, and frequently reconsidered. Times are unique - you'll not take the retirement planning proposal of a speculation consultant as gospel when it includes monetary retirement arranging. You might want to mentor yourself and assume responsibility for your money. If you find concocting for your retirement needs a terrifying assignment, there are numerous retirements arranging instruments you'll flip to for encouragement. These instruments incorporate elegantly composed books that may put forth a defense for the distinction between things like securities and stock, and so on. There are distinct classifications and workshops that you'll take to help you create your retirement venture mastermind to arrive at the objectives you set for your retirement. You don't have to search out transient past the point of no return that you need more cash to cover your retirement needs.

You should instruct yourself to accomplish comprehension of what is achievable with the cash you contribute. For the most part, a reasonable retirement reserve funds organize should accept interests in depository charges, money market and bank account to supply available money; stocks in minuscule, medium, and monster firms for development and appreciation; and different ventures, for example, land for since quite a while ago run preference. Your monetary retirement arrangement should consider the number of years you have left until you expect to resign. You must theorize your cash a ton of years, a great deal of danger you should take with your speculation money. It would help if you had extra of your speculation assets in promptly reachable cash on the off chance you have a couple of years before resigning. You would prefer not to be at retirement's entryway with the vast majority of your money swore in the securities exchange to work out a colossal bit of the cash vanish in a real market plunge, which can occur whenever. On the off chance that you do have numerous prior years of retirement, forceful stocks and land will be a sound venture. Your savings may develop quicker with this speculation procedure because the assets are protected from bound charges, and because of land, it could be tricky to support against swelling. Monetary retirement arranging isn't advanced science. It's to a great extent sense. Besides various retirement arranging instruments, you can use them to assist you with making the most straightforward retirement reserve funds set up for you.

Be that as it may, even the best spread out set up needs to be audited and changed with the conditions. Audit your retirement venture portfolio at any rate yearly and make changes as justified. Try not to let present moment good and bad times in the market lose you your way that prompts your objectives. Good and bad times inside the venture market are essential for the typical pattern of contributing. Adhere to your educated long-haul plans, and like this, the knocks end route should provide all levels out over the years to deliver for your retirement needs. With people living longer, they need to set up well if they need to proceed with how to deal with their life before retirement.

Picking the right retirement plans should exemplify an investigation of your expected retirement costs. These costs could be entirely unexpected for each individual, and the best orchestration of your retirement can permit you to set aside the amount of cash that you hope to require once you select to resign. A few plans may not give speculation decisions that can offer the rebound needed to prevail in the necessary record balance.

Ensure that you essentially embrace the entirety of the potential costs confronted once retirement; else, you'll pick a set up that misses the mark. Your Anticipated Plan Contributions Each Year - The location you choose should issue your yearly expected commitments and assurance that your retirement objectives will be accomplished. A few plans may restrict reasonable obligations to a little sum on a yearly premise, and a few projects may permit make up for lost time commitments once you get close to retirement age. Finding the least complicated retirement plans should accept the gifted duty proposal. The outcomes of helpless retirement arranging will be huge duty liabilities when your payment is required the most. A few methods use pretax commitments that are burdened upon circulation, while elective plans use promises made on a when-charge premise; accordingly, withdrawals aren't loaded after retirement. Duty suggestions will encourage you to select the legitimate designs for all your retirement wants and objectives. Before favoring the best set up for your cash security all through retirement, you'll need to frame a posting of your retirement objectives. Would you be able to wish to travel? Will you keep the next home? Will, you're utilized at a half-time work or take up a diversion with related costs? Your retirement objectives can influence the best arrangement for your future and the measure of retirement pay you'll need to live on while not monetary issues while resigning.

Chapter 2

Your Valuable Resource: The Road to Financial Freedom

The Road to Financial Freedom can ordinarily seem intense to the lookout. An unimaginable measure of examination has been done, and the number of books composed visiting cash opportunity is too various even to consider checking. A few people are battling to get by, and money related freedom is just a fantasy for some in our present economy. What explicitly is cash opportunity and what are the means expected to accomplish it? A simple definition for cash opportunity may be "having a pay cash stream that will cover your everyday costs past your normal life." In elective words, figure your total costs, along with every one of you mounted prices and your assessment's duty and your day-by-day everyday expenses, and so forth, compounded for expansion over your average life expectancy, and contrast that with your projected cash payments over a similar period. You'll have the option to say you have accomplished financial opportunity if your pay surpasses your costs. Extra just, if your income exceeds your liabilities over your usual time, you've achieved economic opportunity. Will this truly be accomplished, or is it every one of an unrealistic fantasy?

The way to cash opportunity isn't a fantasy anyway, a tangible reality, and will be achieved through cautious concocting and execution.

• Troublesome occasions set out open doors for fortunes to be made. You few will consider us to be times as being inconvenient. These days, the web and net advancing freedoms have made way for making abundance like no elective time ever.

• This is regularly like this because they have made it achievable to split second across the world, growing likely clients and customers to levels at no other time feasible. The confirmation lies in the various moguls and tycoons whose fortunes have been immediately made in horrendously late history. These individuals aren't super people anyway, people who followed an organization that place them onto the way to cash opportunity.

• The means they took are not mysteries. They're determined advances which a few people neglect to see over their day by day lives. Independence from the rat race might be a word that has taken power in the twenty-first century.

• It is a term that portrays a lifestyle that is naturally arranged where nobody is needed to work for money to cover their costs. Money-related opportunity propagates that one can be liberated from money duties since he has set a day-to-day existence characterizing set up to deal with his accounts. This idea won't imply that one is released from the obligation.

• Nonetheless, it battles that obligation will be sketched out as a cost. While commitment could be a consistent financial idea, one who has gained independence from the rat race is permitted to check obligation as a portion of his costs rather than a load to his cash objectives. Being monetarily free is a misinterpretation of being affluent.

While we tend to comprehend that wealthy individuals have a scope of million dollars in the record, their overhead since quite a while ago run expenses may imply that they are not as monetarily independent as they show up.

Like this, this idea is an idea receptive to your way of life and the measure of cash you must cover. In this demeanor, cash opportunity isn't as debilitating to acknowledge as first envisioned. Money related Freedom is Time Freedom For various people, to be monetarily free is, for example, having an extended recreation time. The idea of your opportunity is money becomes an integral factor. In all actuality, a monetarily free individual can see that cash is time. When you're in a situation to build up a feeling of your time opportunity, at that point, that implies you're a perfect way to aggregate monetary autonomy. This rule focuses on one's accounts less. Laid out unexpectedly, money related opportunity grants someone to require some investment in exercises without exchanging your available time for money. It relies on tradable resources that compound after some time to cover typical costs. Hence, abundance is framed, which creates more money and time. It permits individuals to cut their working hours with no deficiency of pay because of these days' money-making exercises. This thought requires a great outlook. In our exemplary staff schooling, we are educated to work for cash. Subsequently, we will give in time something to do, and afterward, we get our pay. This can be the renowned time for cash trade.

Notwithstanding, financial opportunity eliminates the idea of your time-and-cash marketing and allows a person to make money work for them. Accomplishing this standing includes an extraordinary move in the way of life and general outlook. While it's not difficult to consider having an ideal opportunity to contribute and do a business, most work environment representatives notice that however much time they have should be put into everyday practice.

A fundamental advance in accomplishing monetary autonomy understands that there are ways to utilize one's time better. To achieve cash opportunity, real mentalities concerning the idea of cash might want to be adjusted. Understanding that money is exclusively an intend to accomplish an end is one factor. Realizing that no one ought to be judged relying upon the measure of cash they own is another. Deciding on this opportunity as the extent of money held annihilates the point because, at the top, you may not accomplish this if you are not content with the cash that you have. Recall that this idea is moreover a unique insight. This discernment is exceptionally associated with the degree of fulfillment that money brings. On another aspect of the coin, we tend to should likewise eliminate the negative impression of cash.

2.1 Dreaming of Financial Freedom or Awake All Night Worrying?

Though the old chestnut that "money is the premise of all underhanded" looks pertinent, imagining that this is ceaselessly the case can offer an anti-agent read about making abundance. Always place into the heart that independence from the rat race could be a substantial undertaking to one feels it is morally stable to frame money. Eventually, having the right disposition about cash will go an all-encompassing technique intending to an entirely unexpected impression of this thought.

Cash opportunity is eventually a viewpoint. The feeling of independence from the rat race for, by far, most people on the planet change. It's the thought of done agonizing over cash duties or questions. Possibly it implies that you have no more obligation and you had the option to take an unrehearsed excursion alongside your friends and family while not telling you're exhausted underneath paid chief and having him advise you, "No!", because of the corporate needs higher numbers.

Perhaps you have fears about bills piling up and evading charge authorities by revealing to them that you get paid one week from now practically in this manner, you'll have the option to have your telephone quit ringing multiple times consistently. A few people may feel independence from the rat race as having the opportunity to purchase that extravagant vehicle, the home they had always wanted, or looking for outlandish extravagances. Being monetarily free is the vibe of security by and by and later on. You can accomplish this by contributing to make a comfortable heap of riches. Eventually, what it recommends that to possess opportunity fluctuates from individual to person. People go through money at astonishing rates.

Everyone utilizes cash, and each one unexpectedly deals with their money. Due to those inconsistencies, independence from the rat race is accomplished from numerous points of view. The prospect of financial opportunity lay on rapidly developing your information concerning back. This data is acquired by perusing elegantly composed enlightening articles concerning this subject. Some may not be in a situation to characterize financial opportunity. By perusing changed articles inside the territories of interests will limit your pursuit; accordingly, you'll have the option to get closer to your objectives.

You'll have the option to see numerous articles on the web that can be of pleasant worth showing you approaches to return up with creative plans to help discover cash ecstasy and figure out your arrangement of what it proposes to be monetarily independent. Elegantly composed enlightening articles can cowl large choice subjects. Many items can depict what money related opportunity is and why just concerning everybody on the planet is endeavoring to achieve it. Elective compositions are instructional exercises that give you the direction to find your natural thought independence from the rat race. Perusing and applying what you read in great instructive articles can help you with invalidating doubts that you'll have and give you the strength and assurance to accomplish a monetarily free way of life. Achieving the predetermined independence from the rat race could appear to be unreachable from the start. While teaching yourself with reasonable useful articles, you might have the option to begin venturing out to colossal abundance. I wager a larger part of the people on the planet has procured freedom all alone without the assistance of late money pass down from grandpa or some new money trust store. I accept any regular person can accomplish cash opportunities.

It essentially comes down to finding and leaning toward the right way to expect you to your future fortunes. It is difficult to arrive at independence from the rat race without seeing a pleasant possibility that will train you and reason to the path cleared in gold. These educational financial articles' assortments will offer you points of interest of various projects like this that you can understand that suits you because not all projects are done similarly.

It would help if you targeted finding a program that is a good counterpart for your cash circumstance and wants. This pined for the thought of monetary freedom may show up kind of a distant dream. Nonetheless, a ton of you filters the extra data you acquire and the self-importance when settling on a choice on what road you might want to go down to gather your fantasy of financial opportunity. My recommendation about turning out to be monetarily independent is to be pretty much as educated as could be expected. Perusing savvy elegantly composed educational articles will encourage you to accomplish your fantasies about being separate from the rat race.

Chapter 3

I Did Nothing Today but Still Got Paid: Passive Income

The average cost for essential items keeps on going up a year in, year out. Be that as it may, let's be honest, our wages aren't filling to a similar extent. What happens these days is that a few of us need to take on a few positions to have the option to save loads of up for the since quite a while ago. In truth, a few people need to take on a couple of to three positions to endure. Tragically, we all are given a similar scope of hours every day - 24. On the off chance that we tackle different situations, prepare to be blown away. Our 24 hours stay 24 hours, and like this, an ideal opportunity for rest and family is undermined. Working longer hours and a ton of occupations can now and again ensure more pay. In any case, a period comes when you'll start asking inquiries. Is it very worth it? How far do you must go until the considerable exertion and unbearable work you contribute through your sweat and difficult work start to exceed the advantages you harvest? At which reason do you pause and understand that the sheer power of your responsibility is going to deliver your pay irrelevantly? While this degree of commitment and diligence is generally praiseworthy, it's conjointly not normal nowadays.

• This is frequently explicitly why you should search for substitute techniques, where your debilitating work will be designed for building a business, accordingly making it at last result for you. The products of your work should benefit you, and you at first.

• Think about all the influential people these days and each one of those before them through the ages. Endeavor and picture what sort of the point of view and standpoint they had throughout everyday life. Believe it or not, the arrangement is evident.

• Except for these to the estate conceived, those people were rarely languid; they couldn't be. These individuals had their needs right and knew explicitly were to coordinate their energy - into making their business work for them.

• They chose to make an inventory of pay all alone instead of putting valuable hours into an impasse work never bound to travel excessively to such an extent. Is there a way to deal with bring in a ton of money without working a lot of hours consistently? Indeed, there's. It's known as easy revenue.

This can be not a left your place of employment and-get-rich-right-now sorts of the answer, anyway a substitution way to continuously flip to, a way that will prompt thriving as well. At the possibility of sounding too coarse, simple endurance isn't any approach to go through life, especially as of now whenever a universe of chance is just before us. Easy revenue essentially implies that you bring in your cash or assets to work for you. Easy payment, at the center, grants you to bring in much money without accomplishing a lot of work.

While it could require a tad of exertion and time toward the beginning, that won't be the case once your easy revenue framework is ready for action. You'll be working less and acquiring a great deal of. Even though making advancement and setting up an effective automated revenue business could be a requesting task, from the start, it can take care of later. Opportunity, autonomy, and everything except full administration of your own time is a portion of the advantages of such an undertaking. In truth, the initial moves towards your easy revenue framework will require work, normally even laborious work; anyway, the top objective makes it all advantageous. One way of needing at it very well maybe this: inside a year, with reliable exertion, you'll be well on your street to both opportunity and security.

Numerous people work an entire lifetime towards this objective, exclusively to accomplish it at past age. The world wherein we will, in general, end up today is progressively overwhelmed by innovation. A few voices caution of creation "holding onto our positions," underestimating human exertion and work, anyway they are neglecting to decide the vast picture. What's a great deal of, who'd wish a burdensome, meticulous occupation in any case, if a substitute can be to pull in that cash from the solace of your comfortable chair? With persistent, innovative advances come entirely different business sectors, thus a full range of pay sources, along these lines effectively available to millions. Specifically, we'll be taking a gander at online wellsprings of easy revenue in this book. You'll figure out how to attempt to utilize Kindle independently publishing, Amazon FBA, specialty sites, subsidiary advertising, email showcasing, and online seminars on Udemy. These frameworks needn't bother with' a ton of in speculations via capital.

You'll need to place in the work toward the start and voyage from that point when all are fully operational. Back once, we were simply adolescents, a great deal of us were encouraged that it is smarter to attempt our schoolwork while we returned home. Why? We tend to possess extra energy for appreciating later, and we will have no concerns concerning our commitments destroying our good times. Not to say, there would be none of those horrendous minutes when time's expiring and you get yourself knee-somewhere down in tasks. Indeed, easy revenue might be a load like getting your work done when you are home.

You'll put inside the work straight away, yet with the point of having a ton of time to loosen up later. Things being what they are, would you say you are readied? In case you're, flip the page, and how about we start. Easy revenue is one that you acquire while not doing a great deal of work or working impressively less, i.e., while being "inactive." Dynamic pay is that the compensation you procure from being utilized. Automated revenue is revenue in your bank stores or interests in Treasury bills. Emotional pay is the expert expense you procure for delivering consultancy administrations. Easy payment is acquiring rental income from the condo unit you are renting out. It is money trickling into your pocket from an (in a perfect world) self-ruling framework you have set up. Dynamic necessities work. Inactive conditions, little or none in any regard. Acquiring an active business is moreover less work than

3.1 Welcome to Passive Income World. It Sucks. You're Gonne Love it!

Beginning an online business and transforming it into monetarily free is presently a reasonable suggestion for any individual who includes a PC and net access. Of a wide range of manners by which to go concerning doing this, some will offer a reasonable return for your endeavors, anyway lamentably, numerous online organizations don't succeed, and people are working them neglect to procure enough to make it beneficial. There are multiple cases where someone has composed an eBook, uncovered it, or opened an online retail location, to search out there aren't any supporters the best way to shape money anyplace is to have to pay clients; the stunt is the way to get them. There are some reasonable manners by which to get clients or traffic to your site. This book is about profitable demonstrated strategies that you'll have the option to use to assemble all-encompassing term easy revenue from the web.

A portion of the things that worked a few years prior is presently not practical because the net is continually changing, developing, and advancing. With 3.5 billion existing clients utilizing the web day by day and another three billion likely clients in Africa, India, China, and the remainder of Asia, the sky is the breaking point for shiny new organizations and an endless pay source. Presently is the reasonable chance to get them in this manner known as "money-making machine." You might want traffic, quality substance, and be set up to attempt actual work (frequently rather than a ton of work). Yet, merely accomplishing the job isn't any assurance of achievement; you must be working in the appropriate regions and doing the right things. Living from an "easy revenue," as it's called, could be a term presently used to portray the pay people get from the web. It's alluded to as easy revenue because, in principle, a large portion of the work is pre-done, and afterward, you pause for a moment and procure the upsides of your work with little work included. In the notice, any online business can require progressing support. The sum required relies upon the situating, its application, and the item you're providing.

There are numerous astonishing styles of web organizations beginning from individuals who require a regular contribution to some that are entirely mechanized. Some web organizations are reasonable and down to earth ways that to bring in money on the web. A few people have kept in touch with some unique licensed innovation, for example, an eBook, an online course, blog entries, or comparable, at that point established an online store to advance their item. Whether they're made or made by the administrator or gained from various sources, there is a considerable measure of your time and energy expected to arrange the situating and tweak it.

When this is done and your site has gone life, you will at that point need to play out various showcasing undertakings like advancing your site or posts and associating with people via online media. Finding similar destinations or places and giving quality input and remarks could be a pleasant technique to advertise your site insofar as it's done in a positive methodology. A good blog or site has new quality substance added consistently to urge people to continue to return at that point, not just preloaded with sense and left to deteriorate. A significant part of the material in a very blog or site can return from another person you recruit to compose the post for you. Yet, you're the person who needs to alter them, plan them, and manage the entire activity.

Suppose you need to take the time and adapt to frame a dream like the one on top of. In that case, it is a sensible way to make an easy revenue for some time, even though you need to live with yourself realizing you are just ripping people off (typically urgent people who can't manage the cost of it). There is little inquiry that a couple of individuals will make a direct dollar on the net. Anyway, a great many people can battle at first, thinking that it's relentless to frame equivalent to you would on the off chance that you had a conventional work. In any case, if you are set up to put in the time and energy required, it is a keen and sound technique to supply a sick long haul pay.

Building a strong since quite a while ago runs easy revenue on the web needs numerous things; the most significant is having traffic. Traffic is the term used to portray the people coming or visiting your site. It's a simple recipe: a ton of people who visit your site, the extra money you'll have the option to make; no traffic, no cash, full stop. It doesn't make any difference how brilliant or how modest your item or administration offer is. If there's nobody to work out it, at that point, nobody can get it. The second extremely fundamental thing makes them think different people need and will pay you to get it. The following essential factor is your believability on the web. This, similar to traffic, will take as much time as necessary to make up, yet there are a few different ways to rush it up. You'll have the option to buy a mailing drill down the web with hundreds and usually a great many email addresses, yet these are common of little cost for a few reasons. These rundowns are past and have been utilized by numerous people to sell their stuff; accordingly, the reaction level is low.

The contrary explanation these rundowns are of questionable worth is because of your smarter to endeavor and gain quality leads of individuals who have communicated an interest in regardless of you are giving instead of merely terminating messages that can complete in many people's spam or garbage mail records. If it even moves beyond their spam blockers. This book can investigate thirty entirely unexpected strategies to making an all-encompassing term easy revenue. It can educate you concerning some of their tremendous and hazardous focuses, advantages, and drawbacks, so you'll make an educated choice on the best methodology for you to continue.

3.2 Passive Income: Such Beauty, Such Grace

Most people concur that the way to progress is determination. They are reluctant to initiate behind the race. These proactive people have demonstrated to get steady in their life. Then again, the apathetic don't have any issue just because they don't have anything moreover. Such people have decided to be subsequently. It sounds reasonable, isn't that right?

Notwithstanding, this balance is that a relic of past times. On the off chance that this can be our attitude, we will, in general, can be shocked at the incredible fortune of the individuals who have applied less exertion and at the disappointment of individuals who have given a valiant effort. It doesn't imply that life is out of line. In truth, we tend to acquire what we do and what we will, in general, don't do. The previous is alluded to as dynamic pay; the last mentioned, uninvolved. Emotional payment is pay we will, in available produce from our arduous work. At the point when we will, in general, work for money, it's dynamic pay. In any case, when it is our own money that works for us, it is easy revenue. Easy revenue is a payment we will, in general, create from our speculation.

Step by step instructions to create automated revenue without dynamic mediation is not a sort of sorcery that everyone may have. How to make automatic payments? Comfortable income is created when our venture procures due to our reasonable choice. At such a price, we tend to are obtained the decision we will in general form and for the danger we will get in available take. When we become terrified of contributing, we tend to tend not to settle on any decision.

Therefore, nothing happens to our cash. To get easy revenue, we should settle on the legitimate choice on what and when to contribute and not choose concerning not contributing. In general, we will ought to conjointly compute the danger - the higher the threat, the upper the come. The lower the opportunity implies that, the more it takes to get the expected return. It relies upon who we tend to are and what venture accommodates our character. Proactive people usually are professionally situated accordingly. They can effectively produce dynamic pay. On the contrary hand, tolerant individuals are astute chiefs and daring people. At present, the inquiry is which kind of workers we should be.

Dynamic workers have full administration of how plentiful they may procure. Anyway, there's a cut-off in the amount as there's a breaking point in their energy and time. In the end, when they stop, so will their pay. In any case, latent workers are extra productive as in they get delighted from the limitless capability of acquiring high with less energy. Additionally, aloof workers can be both dynamic and detached workers. Automated revenue is a great deal worthwhile. It isn't annoying to realize how to get automatic payment.

There is a stack of reachable data around us that will assist us with learning start this with. For the most part, we have heard concerning contributing, and among the supported are securities exchange, securities, shared assets, protection, benefits plan, and depository notes. Before donating, it's imperative to examine your decision speculation. We tend to don't should be the handyman. What is significant is that we will, in general, comprehend the opportunity and the capability of the market we need to enter and start small basically for an endeavor.

As time passes, we will acquire insight and dominate the market we will have picked in general. In the coming of innovation, it's gotten simpler to get extra data for any field of try. The web offers various apparatuses we need to get prepared. The chief critical portion of how to get automated revenue is our viewpoint toward the venture. A few people expect that venture is finished to support our everyday needs, which is an off-base idea. Assuming in this way, it isn't a ton of experience. It's work. Our immediate need can exclusively be supported by dynamic pay. To rely upon speculation for day-by-day needs is flighty. We tend to work to live and, in general, contribute because we secure our tomorrow. Genuine financial backers are future situated. They don't explicitly make cash straight away.

Nonetheless, their cash makes them. That is the reason why we choose this condition latently. Everybody's need these days is not quite the same as our need later on. Our quick might want to be replied by our nearby activity, and prompt outcomes make us develop. Yet, automated revenue isn't one thing that should make us grow.

This is one thing that we tend to ought to develop. Consequently, regardless of what we will, in general, procure now is what we will in general need now. Dynamic pay is the impression of what we tend to do as of now. The appropriate demeanor toward automated revenue is to regard it as a different living substance. Dynamic pay is the thing that we tend to require now. Also, a comfortable income is a thing that our venture wants right now. It is the kind of pet that we tend to should raise. What concerning the business? Is it a very dynamic pay or inactive? Genuinely, it's the mix of both.

A financial specialist effectively controls his cash streams to support his every day needs and at the indistinguishable time save some more prominent segment for his business as a different element. Nonetheless, organizations are progressed these days, relying upon their size. Huge organizations are generally claimed by a scope of individuals alluded to as investors. They enlist chiefs and even CEO's to control their tasks effectively.

3.3 Easy Money without Having to Work for It

Ordinarily, they intercede on a large-scale level. In any case, their administration and energy are confined by the critical pay they get each year if their companies persistently develop. For these individuals, these enormous firms are their wellspring of easy revenue. For little money managers, they should apply all their work for their business. They experience difficulty causing their organizations to develop because they conjointly rely upon the dynamic pay from working for their organizations. Would this imply that to get automated revenue, we should have had enormous funding to theorize? Not basically! We tend to will do as such by putting resources into portions of stocks, even in more modest measure of cash.

This is frequently obvious with shared finances that pool special interests in a minuscule amount to make it one enormous speculation. This implies that we tend to create easy revenue like gigantic financial backers. More or less, we should be advised how to get automated payment while keeping up our dynamic pay, not to trade off the harmony between these two assortments of favorable circumstances. Instructions to get automated revenue is to remain our active pay. Before, it was past the creative mind of everyone to frame money without applying some energy or exertion. To the extent we will, in general, accept, fortune lies on our hands.

Hence, at whatever point we tend to hear that it's right now potential to bring in some cash online, we tend to may without a doubt wondering whether or not to accept. A few people ought to have attempted to look at it themselves as of late. In the not so distant past, one in everything about premier standard patterns to make some money through the web was online foreign trade exchanging. Many have attempted it, and I have become uncertain because they are more likely than not picked up for the exercises of some phony merchants. Yet, on the off chance that we thoroughly search the web, we will, in general, could see more believable locales where we tend to might exchange and construct cash. Along these lines, there are genuinely numerous individuals who have begun to put even in a modest quantity of money. Most amateurs may have encountered some unavoidable misfortunes. Some of them may have mixed more capital and started making some money. Whoever has attempted this money-making model, they're fanatical about automated online revenue. Unfortunately, one will bring in money through the net. There are shifted techniques for building an easy online payment.

The well-known principle pattern at present is through member selling. If we tend to hear these words, the critical impression may be that this can be simply one more online selling plan if not a trick. This can be genuine anyway. This is frequently more than basically selling. This is a real business. To start with the up phase of such online business, we should pay our time, cash, and energy.

What's more, usually, we need to make a few finishes. A partner is an individual who will promote and sell the result of the situating property holders who are envisioning any individual who will do such. Be that as it may, it's not the same as fieldwork selling. Member selling won't compel anybody to figure outside their home. Even though it needs the production of a site or online journals, participation in many gatherings, and article advancing, this is frequently not perpetual because when everything is equipped, your destinations will wrap up for you like a robot serving its lord. Online automated revenue is made when an acquisition of an online item happens. Members will expand automatic online payment in an incredible scope of ways that. One regular model is proposed that of article composing. You may manage and present your reports to various article indexes.

However, remember that you should submit one unique article just a single time because any further accommodation of the duplicate of a similar report to another site is considered spam. You'll compose another comparable spun essay. In our paper, we could embed a few connections that can guide the visitors to your site. The substance of your items won't need to appear to be a direct mail advertisement. It ought to be enlightening in this way that it could pull in more guests. Indeed, even the substance of the articles may affirm the traffic. Utilizing some compelling watchwords to enhance the web index, visitors who may compose similar words in your articles will want to decide your papers inside the query items. The target of article showcasing ought to be to drive traffic to your site with your articles' assistance.

Remember that it's not the post that is important. The peruses ought to recognize you in your field of ability. At the point when you build up your validity, the peruses may follow you and your connection. Writing for a blog could likewise assist you with getting the positioning inside the web index results. Typically, a blog entry or a piece you make probably won't rank inside the web crawler results. Regardless of catchphrases, you remember for your articles to improve the internet searcher, it will not seem to figure for you. It is suggested that you virtually join a few gatherings in a few high-positioning sites along these lines. If feasible, you ought to present a few articles to them. There are different ways you should never really up automated online revenue. You will exclusively start to procure if your site has some traffic.

To make it happen needs time and energy. In the principal stage, you're essentially starting to fabricate the profile that could draw individual visitors to be told a ton of for you and your product. In this manner, manufacturing easy online revenue is not a straightforward occupation in the beginning because the beginning consistently takes long.

3.4 The Master Key to Wealth Creation and Financial Freedom

The first step is to perceive what passive income is and how it differs from the payment you earn operating an hourly or salaried job. The differences are essential as a result of they point to the approach to monetary freedom. If you wish to be your boss and the master of your destiny, passive income is the means to do it. Even if you utilize a different term to describe it, you already understand what active income is. Active income is the type of payment that requires you to actively interact in work for a collection time before you earn it. For example, if you have employment that pays you by the hour, you receive money only for the hours you work. That's active income because your activity is required consistently if you wish to earn a living. An equivalent is real of employment where you make a salary. You are expected to try to abound work in exchange for your compensation.

You must show up at work on time, work a group range of hours, and complete the duties that are half of your job description to earn your salary. You will even be required to perform additional hours without further pay if you're an employee with exempt status. Finally, freelance work additionally qualifies as active income. The freelance staff gets paid only for the work they complete. If they get sick and are unable to finish a task or job, they earn nothing. Currently, let's distinction that from passive income.

Passive income is income that may need some work to line up. However, once you've established a passive income stream, it typically needs only minimum maintenance to keep the money flowing. Let's study a simple example. If you write an eBook, you must pay time and energy to write it. You have to hire an editor and somebody to design the book's cowl, and you will have to form positive that it's in the proper format to sell on Amazon. However, once the book is completed and for sale on Amazon's website, you will earn money every time someone buys it. That's what makes the income passive. If someone buys a copy while you are on vacation or asleep, you still earn cash. I hope you are starting to determine why passive income is the answer to achieving money freedom. Instead of adding more hours to your workday, passive income can make it potential for you to figure fewer hours and still earn a living.

3.5 Why Passive Income matters

Presently we should talk about why having wellsprings of easy revenue is so essential. The ordinary individual won't procure an immense compensation. Valid, a chosen handful of people, acquire tremendous pay rates as CEOs or in various high govt positions. Others may be popular advisors who can charge enormous hourly rates. For the mass individuals, however, our pay potential isn't tremendous. We tend to are confined by our schooling, experience, and the number of hours that we will genuinely (and intellectually) save for work.

Automated revenue discharge prospects that may not in any case exist. It permits us to bring in money in manners that don't need long stretches of additional exertion on a continuous premise - and that is immense. If you find that working extended periods deciphers to having just a limited amount of time with your family - or that you are leaving behind freedoms to attempt to do what you're enthused about - at that point, easy revenue can make the distinction.

Easy revenue matters because it's such a pay that can, without much of a stretch, enhance your dynamic compensation - and in the long run, it may even supplant your active income. Your profit with emotional pay is limited, dependent on the number of hours you're utilized, besides your schooling and work history. There are no such constraints on easy revenue. You have unlimited oversight over it, which implies that no one will cover it. The reality that you'll have the option to acquire it though you are resting, playing along with your youngsters, or on the green implies that you have the freedom to do what you please with your time. As you'll have the option to see, easy revenue contrasts essentially from dynamic pay. Money is money; anyway, the cash you acquire from easy revenue streams is the kind of money that can liberate you from the monotonous routine and permit you to seek after the things that are generally important to you. In the next section, we will talk about the preferences and dangers of easy revenue in more prominent detail so that you realize what's in store as you run after fixing easy revenue streams.

3.6 Ways to Earn Passive Income Online

In the next parts, we will generally take a decent report a portion of the superb ways you'll have the option to begin procuring easy revenue through the Internet.

These are Kindle independently publishing, Amazon FBA, specialty site advancing, an offshoot promoting, email showcasing, and online courses like Udemy.

Significantly vaster than the scope of various areas, just getting started on the Internet, is the number of ways wherein you'll move toward every one of them!

With a store of chances additionally come very few things to pay unique mind to, however.

Whether you should hope to dodge or snatch them, we have a propensity tore worried about covering it. Without more ado, we should get into it.

Chapter 4

Keep Calm & Earn Through Amazon: FBA

Amazon FBA - or Fulfilled by Amazon - is a program that permits you to sell your product on Amazon's online store. The satisfaction of orders is potentially the biggest test confronting numerous online business people, yet with FBA, it is a breeze. You'll have the option to store your product in Amazon, who'll be the one to deal with the strategic stuff, for example, warehousing, transportation to shoppers, taking care of once-deals concerns, and give decent client assistance. This opens up a great deal of your opportunity to focus on the main thing - giving proper, worth-for-money items to clients. It very well may be getting clear at this point that Amazon is among the leaders with regards to introducing new and profoundly open business openings for nearly anybody to benefit from.

This chapter will walk you through everything you need to know to start fulfilled by Amazon for your passive income.

4.1 Step by Step

To begin selling on Amazon, there are several steps to take:

•   Sign Up For Amazon Seller Account. Getting a "seller" account from Amazon is the first step. There are two kinds of performance for the seller - "individual" and "professional" It is free for individuals and allows you to "list" items that already exist in the Amazon catalog. Each time a product is sold, you pay a small fee.

•   This gives you the ability to * create * barcodes for GS1. They come in two formats: UPC (Universal Product Code) and EAN (Universal Product Code) (European Article Number). While these can be purchased relatively cheaply ($10), for standardization, Amazon, Google, and eBay strongly recommend using GS1. You can have your products recognized by the likes of Amazon by using GS1.

•   Create a Legal Company (Optional) You will need a legal business if you are looking to set up a simple FBA operation (and bank account). It allows you to manage taxes better, apart from giving Amazon the ability to open a business account (which is notoriously bad for investing your own money in a personal capacity).

- You then need to get a set of boxed versions of the item. Buy/Build Boxed Products You need to get them into standardized boxes if you create the product yourself. Because there are so many ways to do this, we'll just say that you should look for a boxing/printing company to handle it for you. There are many capable ones.

- Send the products to Amazon You need to send them to Amazon once you've got the boxed products. This is arranged through the Amazon seller system; enabling you to choose when at the Amazon warehouse the products should be received. Again, due to the level of variation in the process, it's best to say that you should follow the Amazon guidelines to do this.

Start Selling. This is the hardest part, which is explained below.

The FBA program might be a magnificent illustration of essentially how a ton of innovation, fundamentally the Internet, totally influences our capacity to learn our own business. Consider how plentiful you'll have the option to improve and unite your undertaking on the off chance that you are unburdened of the preeminent requesting main jobs, which I've expressed, are at times the coordination. The new opportunity in your timetable will give sufficient time for acquisition of product and extending the choice of your variety, setting up associations with quality providers, and so on. This is an excellent and gigantic preferred position from the very get-go contrasted with elective implies that of online deals. It is unbelievable to understand that we tend to live during a period where a little business, as little as interest even, can just join and begin helping out an aggregate that is Amazon. What's more, not just coordinate, anyway, straightforwardly receive the rewards of their incredible foundation to propel your pay.

4.2 Amazon FBA Vs. An Online Store

Besides dealing with the strategic stuff, there are different reasons why Amazon FBA is better than fitting and dealing with your online store. The first is a quicker conveyance. With Amazon's broad market reach and calculated capacities, it doesn't take long for your staff to desire your clients. Difference this with doing the delivery yourself. Not exclusively will this encourage to more readily fulfill your clients, anyway quick transportation conjointly extends the variety of product you'll sell? Time-delicate products that may terminate, or in any case endure on account of delayed delivery measures, are one such model. With an assurance of a particularly spectacular undertaking, speedy shipments are a preferred position barely procured when you're out there without help from anyone else.

Second, FBA gives your item altogether a ton of openness than if you'd retail it to you all alone. It's because Amazon is the most significant online retailer on the planet - considerably more substantial than most option actual retailers! By having your item on Amazon FBA, you get delighted from excellent higher permeability and, most likely, extensively a larger number of deals than if you'd do it in your online store. Complete autonomy could have an appeal, anyway setting up a look and making standing for yourself may require a long ton of cumbersome work and responsibility. Aside from being debilitating, the dangers and possibilities of disappointment if you are going it single-handedly are considerably more significant. Seeing as you're perusing a book on automated revenue, you likely aren't very energetic concerning the real possibility of placing long stretches of work into an endeavor that won't take care of itself. Third, making your item realistic on Amazon's FBA grants your clients profit from its free transportation within a couple of days and diverse comparative conveyance decisions. Once more, this can be a favorable strategic position you can use to sell your items productively. Besides, this and various advantages offered to Amazon clients are among the reasons that this stage appreciates an extensive customer base worldwide. This can be explicitly how this general gainful framework works significantly implies that it gives all gatherings their cake cut. Finally, FBA offers you - as an online dealer - a great deal of required validity because of just put, Amazon is one among the chief confided in brands in the globe.

Will you envision that it is so valuable to piggyback on the standing of 1 like Amazon? Dazzling, right? This takes us back to the subject of making standing for yourself as an online retailer, as this progression of the methods is not trouble on FBA.

Usually, you require you to get positive input and guarantee a happy customer base, yet the degree in that FBA encourages this strategy is truly important. Should any issues emerge after the shipment, Amazon's profoundly talented workers will deal with their customer administrations' completion and any common grievances or apprehensions. As route as supporters are concerned, they are managing Amazon. At the same time, you become an integral factor as an outsider that gives the item and is vouched for by the eminent Amazon Company.

4.3 Product is Key. Don't Panic Keep Hunting Right Product

Selling the right item is the absolute most essential factor for prevailing on FBA. These are generally less expensive, effectively sent items with negligible dangers related to transport. Your articles should be referred to as items that show up quickly and inside the guaranteed condition. This can be tougher to accomplish with bound sorts of papers, subsequently be aware of what you might want to get into, especially in the beginning! In this way, what are the things to mull over to show up at the "right" item? These incorporate, among others: Ideally, the product should be inside the $10 to $fifty fluctuate. Such a thing sells the most and is the simplest to sell. This shift is just about perpetually a great deal of or less a specific value pass to progress, along these lines commonly denote the suitable spot to begin your business. Weight: Your items should weigh as light-weight as potential. Generally, inside the interest of transportation, putting away, and so forth, the lighter product can esteem you less in these regions. Less expensive coordination's aren't the sole motivation to go for light-weight items, however. The less they gauge, the less likely they're to be delicate; hence the chance of any common issues with transport is significantly decreased. Rivalry: Like elsewhere where selling happens, FBA might be a commercial center like each other regarding rivalry. Decide whether you have any actual and potential item rivalry among the prime five,00zero hit rank, or BSR in your item's essential classification. Likewise, ensure that you don't have rivalry from notable names in your picked specialty or class, as this is regularly a strong rivalry executioner.

It is generally a decent arrangement to stay eliminated from the giant fish, particularly if you're the tenderfoot. Packed, cornered, or in any case, full business sectors or specialties are something else to evade. Another side of the opposition you need to look at is that the surveys. The extra audits they need, particularly sure ones, the more significant is that the resistance and subsequently, the test of breaking into the market. The off chance that the audits on contending items are under fifty demonstrates a genuinely decent probability of breaking that specialty or market. Sturdiness: Whenever feasible, sell stock that doesn't just die. This can limit your dangers for discounts or substitutions, the two of which can impressively affect your edges. Consider the distances your merchandise may go to incite to the client, further because it recommends transport required. Never-endingly ascertain the danger of overseeing bound items, as various them are a terrible dream to dispatch. The smoother the delivery is, the great deal of healthy your base of pay will turn into. Edges: Ideally, your edge (level of benefit over selling worth) ought to be in any event 75 percent to make it worth your time and energy. Continuously keep a watch on the numbers. This can be the soul of your business.

4.4 Fun Fact FBA Success

The superb dealers on Amazon are exceptions, i.e., way unique and separate from the pack's remainder. In general, they will embrace the reasoning that selling on Amazon appreciates securities exchange or monetary standards exchanging. More than that, the following elements have - to a decent degree -

represented their prosperity: Selling a more significant amount of an item is more worth useful - and beneficial - contrasted with selling not many. Selling on Amazon makes economies of scale plentiful simpler because the coordination's are taken care of by a central coordination's behemoth. This is why more modest value ranges are a roadway to progress on FBA and stress 'interstate'! When your framework is ready for action, these items will sell briskly and in enormous volumes. Also, during the time spent getting going, indeed, clearly, it's simpler to hoard a client base through modest and different items. The adaptability and readiness to be accountable for mistakes in judgment and changing appropriately are vital to being adaptable and effective in the area alluded to as Amazon. The inverse essentially makes it impractical for vendors to attempt these items the perfect things at the ideal time for selling Amazon's accomplishment. Not all things go as indicated by setting up always. This is customary. Try to discover from your errors, be capable and continue onward.

Maybe, in particular, you need to self-scrutinize and see the blunders of your ways unmistakably and all alone. These ethics can help you see when and how to adjust and improve your business, which is vital to progress. The best merchants are adequately focused on controlling their inventories, cash streams, and danger quite well. On the off chance that you are caring for business by and by, it is essential to be careful and efficient.

Consider it is dealing with a store, which is carefully the thing you're doing principally. Keeping a clear focus on your objective and having stone-hard will and assurance. This can be how we get places throughout everyday life, and it's no very surprising on FBA. The high Amazon dealers don't mind concerning being off-base or right - they consider making cash. Heaps of it! The best merchants see things from longer periods like quarters or years rather than days or maybe weeks as it were. Indeed, even in different backgrounds and businesses, this is the methodology that most fruitful people assume. It shows that you are preparing to stun the world, are considerable, and see the 10,000-foot view. Moreover, this sort of impression of time causes you to look forward with decent prescience, which could be a pleasant, authoritative ability. If you meticulously and shrewdly consider these elements in starting your Amazon FBA business, you fundamentally increment your odds of bringing in brilliant cash.

Chapter 5

Writing and Selling an E-Book with Kindle Direct Publishing

Encourage Direct Publishing might be a stage where you'll have the option to publish your books at no expense independently. Encourage direct distributing, or KDP is Amazon's independently publishing stage where you can spread your books without much of a stretch, keeping up full oversight over them though simultaneously contacting millions and bunches of peruses around the world. One more brilliant illustration of how the Internet clears the technique for a few impressive individuals; Kindle distributes the composing market more than ever. Whatever you're focused on the field could be, there's almost no restriction to possible achievement from books to manuals. With Amazon's way-extending and global reach, crowds worldwide will rapidly be acquainted with your substance. The previously mentioned command over your meaning is one of the critical edges of this technique. This proposes that any altering, organizing, covers, and so forth are up to you, and you, to control and coordinate the methodology you see fit.

This chapter will walk you through everything you need to know to start Kindle self-publishing for your passive income.

With Kindle direct distributing, you'll procure sovereignties on your work of as much as 70% of the blanket worth of your books. KDP also gives you the adaptability to distribute rapidly, making your books reachable on the Kindle Store at spans a couple of hours or maybe minutes after transferring your material. Will you envision how incredible this might have been years and years prior, or perhaps more as of late? There isn't anything preventing you from distributing a book in no time, for millions to have moment admittance! That is to say, getting your work printed, in addition to making it so accessible, was at one time a genuine cerebral pain for authors. Indeed, that point is no extra. KDP allows you to elevate your books to millions and scores of peruses worldwide with the presence of Amazon.com in virtually all nations. Finally, KDP licenses you to make your books out there for everyone as eBooks that might be check through Kindle gadgets and free Kindle applications though focusing on the environmental factors.

5.1 Step by Step

•   You need to register with Amazon Kindle Direct Publishing to get started to start publishing your writing. It's for free. Using your Amazon username and password to sign-up.

•   Once you're in and have typed out the title of your eBook, you'll be given two steps to complete.

•   The first step is to add book data and upload information, while the second step includes the management of publishing rights, pricing, royalties, and the collection of countries where the book can be bought.

•   You will also be given an option to protect your book's quality, and it is not mandatory to do so.

•   After you have completed all these measures successfully and submitted the book for review, it might take a few days to hear back from Amazon when the page is up and running.

•   You will have to find out the niche, check the right categories to sell if your book is going to sell, do proper research to write a high-quality book, and focus on some promotion and marketing.

•   Though there is a built-in audience at Amazon, it is still essential to get traffic, reviews for your book and help it sell.

5.2 Pros & Cons of Kindle Self-Publishing

Independently publishing, as an implies that of automated revenue, is turning out to be even a great deal of mainstream nowadays. There are a couple of explanations behind this. First, many impediments or passage hindrances that typically face new organizations aren't in independent publishing. What they mean by this is regularly to publish your books on Kindle independently, you don't might want particular programming, you would prefer not to be an influential figure, master or master in a too unequivocal that you wish to record on, you don't might want to do arrange advertising or associated influencers, you don't have to offer to people straightforwardly or address or market, and you would prefer not to pay a whole stack of cash. As a general rule, it is potential to acquire from Kindle independently publishing while not spending anything a great deal of than the expense of your Internet association.

As an issue of truth, not even the unsatisfactory nature of your composed substance can block you from bringing in cash off it. Positively, you should ceaselessly devote your earnest attempts to assembling quality, yet this probably won't be the specific deciding issue in explicit specialties or explicit objective crowds. Contingent upon the circle you might want to cross, your potential peruses may often think more about the composition's substance rather than instructive ability or lingual mastery. The truth that it's so direct to get into independently publishing on Kindle conjointly recommends substantially less danger, or rather, the freedom to face a more significant number of challenges than you may inside the old distributing world. This can be because these stages are not requesting speculation shrewd and permit significantly more space for experimentation and evaluating various specialties, approaches, and styles. Another explanation behind independently publishing the rising notoriety is that it gives an excellent chance to acquire shrewd easy revenue. After you have composed your top-rated book and transferred it to Amazon's Kindle

Store, you watch for deals to stream in. In conclusion, this will give you a gigantic chance for accomplishing notoriety and great pay. Considering that Amazon is available in basically all nations the globe inside the valuable people who get books on the Kindle Store, you have an expanse of chances for accomplishment.

5.3 How to Self-Publish Your First Kindle eBook

The important advance to effectively independently publishing your underlying Kindle eBook is to attempt to do your investigation. The chances of effectively distributing your underlying, and your ensuing, eBooks on the Kindle Store rely exceptionally upon your capacity to know the right specialty or themes to cover. A few independent publishers commit the without a doubt deadly error of expecting that subjects they are appallingly bountiful intrigued or enthusiastic concerning or points that they unequivocally feel can be ahead will fabricate four generally excellent themes to publish books on independently.

As of now, I'm not saying that such subjects are destined to disappointment consequently. While it's brilliant on the off chance that you'll distribute on one thing that you're intrigued or enthusiastic worried about, there is a ton of to effectively independently publishing a book at that point composing on such themes. The way to deciding whether a potential specialty will be beneficial in independent publishing is to pick subjects that numerous people are interested in. By investigating what people wish, you take out the opportunity to fizzle on your first independently publishing attempt. This can be because you'll act naturally distributing dependent on a model that has worked for all organizations since days of yore - offer and request. Like this, while doing your examination, it is essential to show up for designs where you will sell your independently published eBooks - the Amazon Kindle Store.

Consequently, what's it explicitly that you ought to investigate regarding methods? First, examine the various books that cowl or focus on the indistinguishable theme or specialty. Then, assess the places of these and other comparative books among the Kindle store's available deals as the high 100 successes in their classes. In conclusion, look for a commercial center or specialty that is not, in any case, swarmed because those will be those you have an extensively higher likelihood of overwhelming and prevailing in.

Think about both the negative and positive audits, anyway give extra consideration to the negative ones. Negative audits offer you essential bits of knowledge concerning the shortcomings of books that have been distributed on the indistinguishable specialty or subject in front of you that you can fill in or misuse. Fundamentally, negative audits will help you maintain a strategic distance from traps that can undermine your blueprint. Positive audits offer you experiences into what different books have done right, what your potential peruses will value best, and all things considered, what thoughts to more expand on.

You don't need to waste time anyway. You'll have the option to construct the current wheel much better and accomplish independently publishing your underlying eBook on the Kindle Store. At last, after the basis has been set down through adequate exploration, and an arrangement of the pressure has been explained by attempting at surveys, the time has come to move on to the principal work. Since you have made your framework, it's an ideal opportunity to state the book expressly. You'll do that in two manners by which: recruit a professional writer or compose it yourself. If figuring out how to manage a book, extraordinary composing abilities, and skill on a bound theme or specialty are not kidding difficulties for you, at that point, recruiting a professional writer is a way to deal with go. No, I'm not talking concerning employing Casper the Friendly Ghost or another creepy component to do the composition for you anyway real individuals who can genuinely compose well on your picked specialty or points and will move all rights to the written work to you.

5.4 Putting It All Together for Publication

In different words, professional writers are people who will compose your book for you and give all credits due, financial and something else, to you in return for a fixed compensation. You may distribute the book under your name and get all the brilliance, acclaim, and, ideally, sovereignties. So, where would you be able to lease professional writers who'll do the dirty work for you? There are numerous sites you'll have the option to look at, for example, Up-work earlier called an Odes, Elance, and Freelancer.com, among others. Employing professional writers is extremely simple. The test lies in using great ones. You may need to attempt to component due to tirelessness and perhaps request real examples of their work so concerning you to screen out the great journalists from the undesirable ones. One technique you'll have thought about whether or not a planned professional writer is pleasant is by attempting at their profile's shopper input segment.

There, you'll have the option to perceive how their previous buyers feel about the nature of their work. In a similar area, you can get a thought of their average rating. Another technique to ask a review of a point of view professional writers' type is by evaluating how long have they been composing or working for buyers inside the site moreover the number of gigs they dealt with as of now if such data is achievable or available. It's a brilliant way to deal with decide how bountiful composing aptitude they as of now have. Remember that quality ceaselessly includes some significant downfalls. Planned journalists that incredibly low charge rates - contrasted with most different ones at least - could be making some challenging memories getting enough customers to shape a living one methodology or the other. While it is anything but an assurance of helpless composing abilities, probabilities are theirs may not be of sufficiently high quality or that they need more insight notwithstanding. Either way, it is your determination - and hazard. The more recognized independent sites, as Up-work, for example, will encourage you to pull in the type of essayist generally fitting for your financial plan. While setting up your venture, it is conceivable to deliver particulars concerning your situation and assets. The degree of involvement you're searching for or can pay cash for will be introduced in the depiction. What this infers is that you'll have the option to call attention to that you can just acknowledge less aptitude, however for less compensation, and the other way around. This serves to higher represent your conditions and needs to any or every single possible author. Conceded that looking for these administrations comes hazard, follow the means referenced above, and that danger gets negligible. Two exceptionally crucial parts of your eBook are the title and cowl.

While the facts confirm that it's inside that matters, your cover and title are those that can tempt individuals to at least attempt the substance by either "needing" inside or downloading an example. These 2 are the entryways through which individuals might want to enter to decide your book's meaning. If the entryway's ugly, they will not consider looking inside. Each of your cowl and title should stick out and be unique, i.e., eye-getting. Given that the ordinary possibility on Kindle has restricted opportunity to settle on and stores of elective books to kind through, they're going to most you probably pour over the reachable books on Kindle rapidly and accordingly. Your book has a second - in all likelihood, even a brief moment - persuading peruses to interfere with their hoping to try out your book's substance or depictions.

You'll rethink from sites like Fiverr, where all gigs are typically valued at $5.00. The imperative factor is you have just thought of what you need the duvet to respect so the visual craftsman can undoubtedly do the blanket per your determinations. If not, it could take a smidgen of time and go to and from to instigate right. When you complete the duvet, it's an ideal opportunity to deal with your title. Your title gives peruses an arrangement of what your book is about in only a couple of seconds. This can be the place where decent copywriting becomes an integral factor.

Great copywriting will help your hand-off to your potential purchasers what your book's for. Those will be the primary standards by that they will choose whether or not to purchase your book. While it isn't completely essential, advancing your book will fundamentally encourage support deals. You have a few options open, each paid and free. You'll consistently utilize your online media accounts like Facebook and Twitter to advance your book for nothing. For paid other options, you'll use Facebook promotions notwithstanding rethink it using sites like Fiverr.com, among others.

5.5 Must-Know Tips for Writing a Book, the Secrets Revealed

We should start with the composition. Many people don't assume of themselves as essayists. Anyway, genuinely composing is merely putting words along in a significant way. That is something you do throughout the day, every day, regardless of whether you are forming Tweets, chatting on the telephone, or answering an email. A book is only an all-inclusive variant of that. To give you an arrangement of how basic it will be to prompt an eBook up on Amazon, let me share with you the undeniable reality that the ordinary book on the Kindle Store is just about 10,00zero words long. That means close to 32 40 pages of text. That is very little by any stretch of the imagination. You could have a draft of your book in under three weeks on the off chance you composed next to no as 500 words each day. On the off chance that writing is one thing that doesn't return just to you, it might assist with returning up with a nearby diagram first. Taking a gander at the tables of substance in elective books in your picked specialty might be a decent way to incite thoughts regarding what to join. You don't need to purchase the books except if you need to. Many Kindle titles have a "Look Inside" that will allow you to peruse the list of chapters and the essential section or book.

That might be sufficient to concede you a vibe for what you need to join. On the off chance that you are very awkward with composing, you will wish to consider utilizing a discourse to-message device. The advantage of doing that will be that you don't need to record, at least not from the outset. You can pick a subject, talk concerning it, and let the apparatus you utilize interpret it into text. In any case, you will audit the content, right blunders, and work to make a reasonable stream with your substance, yet the basic technique can be direct. Generally, it is more straightforward for someone who doesn't ponder themselves to be an essayist to work with one thing composed than to feel like they need to begin without any preparation with an exact page. At the point when you have an underlying draft written, I emphatically counsel that you set it away for each week or two proceeding endeavoring to overhaul it. Having it delayed off from your venture will help you take a gander at it with a new point of view.

At the point when you are doing bring it out once more, reciting it for all to hear could be a horrendously decent way to deal with spot rehashed words and off-kilter expressing. When we will, in general, sweep quietly, our eyes will appear in available skip words. Reciting for all to hear is also a compelling way to edit and spot homonym use and normal elective slip-ups. Whenever you have changed the book, you should lease an expert supervisor or editor on the off chance that you figure your book may, in any case, contain blunders. There is no disgrace in getting another pair of eyes on your book. It could conjointly help encourage a few people who are proficient about your theme to peruse the book and offer their feelings.

Chapter 6

Sale Your Interest through Niche Websites

A specialty site is focused on a particular objective or term, typically called "watchwords," which web indexes like Google and Bing use to help people scrounge around for stuff on the Internet. Also, for your online easy revenue capacities, it is best your specialty site's catchphrase is one that is very express, extraordinary, or focused on. On the off chance that you desire to figure out how to frame $1000 per month from home, a straightforward way to understand you will likely shape specialty sites, assemble cash on-line from these web properties and flip them for a clean add of cash. A stack of web business visionaries who toe this line of making money online is in a situation to hold over their monetary difficulties effortlessly and rapidly.

For example, suppose you realize how to shape an unmistakable fragment site or blog. In that case, you'll assemble 4 to five areas with the point of developing $200 every month from every one of those minuscule virtual property organizations. Following three months of reliably making easy revenue online from a site, flip it and assemble another as another option. You must follow fundamental advances to begin making specialty sites productively, and I can momentarily put forth a defense for everything about beneath.

This chapter will walk you through everything you need to know to start niche websites for your passive income.

6.1 A Peek into the Guru Mind and Niche Websites

One explanation you'll have to put up an unmistakable portion site for automated revenue reasons for existing is that it's generally useful, i.e., minimal effort, to get ready for action. On the off chance that you'd prefer to accelerate the cycle, you'll pay for administrations and products that can assist you with doing that anyway. As a rule, the sole necessary cost included is acquiring a site name and a Webhosting account, which midpoints between $five to $7 month to month in sync with your choice of host. While it may require some investment and stacks of work to arrange your specialty site, it isn't confounded in any regard. Its general straightforwardness regarding setting up is another shrewd motivation to actuate into specialty site advertising. Another valid justification is the course of the outcome of events.

As referenced before, you may need to put inside the exertion and time, mainly when setting up the site. Also, it won't concoct moment pay, despite what different cynics would have you suspect. In addition to the fact that it takes time to set up your webpage and all that it wants to figure, it will likewise take effort for Google to genuinely see your substance, rank your site in query items for its specialty watchwords, and for significant traffic to get back to your website.

While you can acquire reasonable pay from specialty site selling, it's one that will be very limited. The giveaway here is "specialty, " which implies that position and infers a deep specialization or core interest level. You have fewer possibilities contrasted with extra summed up the items that has a lot bigger business sector. While it's unquestionably potential for you to flip your specialty site into an expert on your unequivocal specialty, the prospects are relatively low, and ultimately, your pay potential can level. You'll alleviate this danger by placing in various specialty sites, which you'll do with the measure of spare time that you'll get joy from once your specialty site's as of now going.

6.2 Building a Niche Website for Novices: It's Easier Than You Think

Prior, we referenced that the essential thing you'll have to do before fitting the specific site is to look out for your specialty. Inability to try to do so may deliver all your persistent effort to place in your area and advance it pointless or squandered because you'll wind up going for an unfruitful specialty. If you wish to see a decent specialty effectively, you may want to move toward it like composing a blog, one where you may want to produce a ton of profitable themes and substance. What's more, similar to Amazon FBA prior, I propose focusing on specialties you are incredibly familiar with or energetic about.

Why? Odds are, you're as of now educated on it. Observe what I mean by focusing on putting it first to read for the benefit and not taking the plunge. It's undoubtedly conceivable that what you're enthusiastic and proficient concerning - say, waste bugs - is not a productive specialty while exemplary vehicles - that you'll not be energetic about as of the moment - could be a beneficial one. In which case, pick the right vehicle's specialty. Focusing on your interests and interest implies that given your absence of information on your distinguished likely specialties' benefit, assess that of the one you are keen on or are enthusiastic for first. If you find that your optimal thing isn't sufficiently productive, don't be reluctant to go with individuals you are not by and proficient about.

Set aside some effort to examine concerning it and acclimate yourself with it. Whenever you have enough essential information, you'll have the option to either investigate more stuff about it to make enough significant substance or re-appropriate it to independent scholars. There's extra than one technique to skin and all things considered potato. Actually, with the expanse of information that is the Internet, you'll have the option to turn out to be knowledgeable in basically any point you can assume of. Some will set aside an extra effort to check other than others. Anyway, it will be done in any case. Once upon a crude time, if an individual wished to get proficient on something, it was either formal schooling or parcels or maybe thousands of hours inside the library. The present status of issues is with the end goal that you'll have the option to learn and, accordingly, make money off your insight from an isolated spot - your seat. You can't anticipate controlling precisely on human minds without formal training and instructing anyway regarding data. The Internet is boundless. In this way, if a specialty you wish to incite is associated with lies past your experience, get to learning and investigating. Assume of it as taking a course of types to ask a task.

6.3 Narrowing Down Your List of Niche Ideas

When you have spread out the entirety of the possibilities and thoughts, all that is left is settling on the appropriate decision. Presently, there is a choice of manners by which to travel concerning this. Anyway, it starts with you having a firm comprehension of how far your data extends in specific regions, your abilities to give content, and so forth. It conjointly makes a choice simpler to possess an away from where you need to take your site and what you want to accomplish. One of the manners in which you'll choose to channel or short-list your specialty thoughts is through the edge volume rules. Business people will be delegated the individuals who favor selling excessive cost low-volume (high edge) items or low-worth-high-volume (low acidity) stock. Each has its arrangements of advantages and disadvantages. Those with significant expenses will give you impressively more prominent overall revenues or spreads per unit of offer; however, you may have to sell less because they are costly.

Interestingly, the low evaluated stock offers you essentially fewer edges and need you to provide more units to think of the indistinguishable amount of pay as selling more extravagant items. Which is ideal? It's everything up to you, contingent upon each's experts and cons as it identifies with the specialty, the thing, and along these lines, the market. Another channel through which you'll limit your rundown of potential specialties is the ability to state many articles or good substance on the thing expressly. A decent benchmark - yet discretionary - is fifty articles to 100 pieces.

Suppose you consider yourself to be able to create that bountiful substance throughout the year. In that case, it implies that you're intrigued or enthusiastic about the specialty and, accordingly, are educated for it. This reveals to you that you will, without a doubt, have enough energy and interest to own this effectively. On the off chance that you can't, consider employing professional writers, which will set you back a great deal after all. Given that hiring consultants are a cost, thus a financial backer's arrangement; you may wish to try not to do hence at first. It's most likely best to put in the additional exertion and turn out as quite a bit content as feasible at the outset. With this methodology, you will accumulate the most extreme measure of capital. With that, you'll have the option to lease help later. Around then, you'll start to put the procedure on autopilot. Knowing whether the specialty has partner advancing projects that pay reasonable commissions is another central question to consider when narrowing down your rundown of specialty ideas.

6.4 A Good Grasp of Knowledge

While there are partner selling programs for anything, isolating the decent ones from the slouches is a proper general guideline for programs that give in any event 10% commission. I focus on around twenty to thirty twenty commission. It very well may be challenging to track down and set up the most productive projects from the outset, obviously, yet you should decidedly set the bar to 10% at any rate. These norms aren't merely viewing trading in for spendable dough as fast as could be expected, anyway conjointly seeing introducing your site as a yearning project rather than a minimal effort, little time leisure activity. Remember that advanced products will surrender higher commissions contrasted with an actual item for one direct explanation - cost. Advanced things can be handily repeated at very tends almost no cost in the smallest degree while actual product involves expenses to raise. This way, in case you're gunning only for big commissions, advanced items could be best for you. Not to say that actual product suck at commissions. I'm essentially saying that while they'll pay reasonable commissions, they're not as high as those given to merchants of advanced items.

More than just shrewd commissions, you may likewise have to look out for tends if a particular specialty is one where individuals truly fabricate money. What benefits is high as can be commissioned on things with nary any clients? Maybe that is the reason they are offering high commissions - they are laborious to sell! Just like that the case with most things throughout everyday life, if it shows up as being too savvy to be valid, at that point possibly it presumably isn't, accurate that's. With all the issue that goes into setting up your site, you would prefer not to discard everything in a useless market! So how might you genuinely get a handle on if people assemble cash in this specialty? Here's the way you'll have the option to do it.

Presently direct a journey on those watchwords that create a lot of traffic and note regular sites that show up on their indexed lists' essential pages. If there are, look at them. If there are no normal ones, only attempt those highest-level locales per watchword search. How might you tell on the off chance that they're making money? A few zones unveil what they are doing; say like the site Kenrockwell.com, whereby he says that the site causes him to uphold his family at the lower part of each page. In any case, most various sites don't attempt this; hence how might you get a thought of if they are making smart money? Market surveys are another methodology of doing as such.

On the off chance that a particular fragment has a few item surveys with associate connections in them, it's a wise sign that maybe individuals are making tight money inside the specialty. Remember that, while a dynamic market implies that probabilities are cash to be made there, it may also mean wild rivalry. Generally, you can get an arrangement if individuals are bringing in money during a particular specialty by attempting to catchphrase search traffic, surveys with subsidiary connections, expensive items, and high commission rates.

6.5 Making Money through Your Niche Website

There are a few different ways that you'll construct money from your specialty site, which embrace direct selling, paid connections, paid promotions, AdSense ads, and partner selling. In the accompanying part, we will bring a look into the planet of subsidiary selling personally. On one last note concerning specialty sites, even though they require significant work to get things fully operational quickly and involve a great deal of danger than is the situation with automated revenue frameworks ordinarily, they're still at the high with regards to automatic revenue potential. Grounded sites that attract massive measures of traffic are among the most self-governing easy revenue attempts.

On the off chance that a site figures out how to make a local area around it, it's apparent that this local area would conceivably take over a large portion of the site's elements. A bit of a ton of adored locales regularly has a client happily expect the jobs of organization, by and large in any event, for nothing! Along these lines, if you perceive what you are doing and set everything up likewise, this is a chance to make a practical living, moneymaking machine.

Chapter 7

Sell Your Experience through UDEMY -Online Courses

Web-based learning keeps on expanding in ubiquity, and Udemy is one in all the significant stages for such. Furthermore, this is for a horrendously legitimate explanation. Regardless of whether to enhance one's conventional training or to offer reparations for the deficiency in that department, this sort of learning is changing into less and less confined every week. This way, it's nothing unexpected that the stages that give unequivocally turned into a productive business, with the possibility to try and turn into an instructive expert on an institutional level later on. Just like that the case with the entirety of the business fixates on the Internet, Udemy also presents a few chances to astute and noteworthy individuals like you. Because of the wide range of learning levels, from section level to profoundly progressed, it's a decent stage to begin if on-line courses are something you need and can make. It doesn't make any difference bountiful if you end up being nevertheless gifted in the picked field. Anyone can set up an online course here. The clients are the individuals who will pass judgment if your period is sufficient or not - reflecting subsequently in your pay or criticism.

As of the beginning of 2016, Udemy has purportedly served a ton of than ten million individuals with over forty,000 courses. At such a rate, this stage can positively acknowledge itself directly at the high of this market appallingly soon. This can be why now is the ideal opportunity to jump aboard with this program and notice a spot for your easy revenue anticipates Udemy. Regardless of whether you are a genuine talent on your subject, instructing regularly goes every way. In the strategy for giving these courses to other people, you might turn out to be more capable and extend your information at the indistinguishable time! We'll take nearer notice of this potential and a couple of essential things to see as you leave on this endeavor.

In this chapter, I will walk you through everything you need to know to start selling your courses on Udemy for your passive income.

7.1 Potential Income: It's Worth it

While top Udemy teachers fabricate a fortune in Udemy, not every person acquires enormous pay. It's cost noticing that a few teachers get $60 month to month; however, the top tip ones can earn vi figures every year. Try not to allow this to debilitate you as this doesn't mean a store of rivalry for you in expression, nor will it imply that the prime is involved. On the off chance that something, it merely goes to show in what manner or capacity much you'll bear this site. On the off chance that a course maker isn't pulling in an incredibly crucial measure of pay, this can be in all likelihood since they either haven't made quality or have decided to show a disagreeable or perhaps too inescapable ability.

On the contrary, those who are drawing six figures have probably worked, depleting for their position, and have arrived at a degree of association and capability that can't be considered typical toward the beginning. Clearly, at that level, they're presumably some a significant organization or, at least, a group of teachers, like this no might want to take a look at yourself to those circles on Udemy, notwithstanding! Either implies, you shouldn't feel too firmly about both of these boundaries. With center, imagination, and due constancy, you can get to precisely where you wish to be.

7.2 Time Frame for Udemy Courses

Making an online course will require a massive load of speculation from you, altogether regarding your time and conceivably assets. For certain people, especially book writers, it takes as much time as composing an undeniable book. It's a lot simpler if you as of now have a book or some other unique material like sites and workshops to begin with, on which you'll have the option to base your course. You can no doubt deliver a system in one two-to 3-hour sitting with such materials available.

However, if you are, for all intents and purposes starting without any preparation, distribute a great deal of your time for it and spending plan such time astutely. Presently, what you are giving is a course. However, this doesn't imply that there can't be some severe pitch snared to it. As an issue of the real world, it could presumably do ponders for your undertaking. You may recollect that learning has ceaselessly been a great deal of power if it had been fun and creative simultaneously on the off chance that you get back to secondary school for ablaze. By utilizing a level of inventiveness when assembling your course, you can even wind up making some great memories yourself! Making the most of your work always helps and will unquestionably allure you to work quicker and be extra time proficient.

7.3 The Usefulness of Udemy

Extra than basically specialized capabilities on the course you will make, you will also want enough video creation abilities to make your video courses. While it's positively potential to utilize your cell phone's camera to film yourself, there's a ton of to it than that. It requires post-shooting alter, sound, and video setting abilities in any event on the off chance that you might want a good video on Udemy. Those are exceptionally specialized things that you'll, in all probability, learn over the long haul; nonetheless, if you need to make a keen course at the soonest expected time, better consider the material and get qualified assistance for the video shoot and alters.

Regardless, this is another chance to utilize the administrations of consultants to help you with your undertaking. There's an abundance of video editors and good blenders working as consultants on-line, and a massive load of them are genuine trained professionals. For this, allude back to independent sites we tend to reference previously, any semblance of Upwork, Freelancer, Elance, and so on. You'll divvy up the errand and tackle the composition or another part of the work, or you'll have the option to designate the fundamental factor to a gifted. Comparative with your spending plan, time, and abilities, you may catch the best how to get ready. On the off chance that you do have natural skills in video altering and impacts, be guaranteed because that private touch exclusively you'll have the option to give may be the factor that makes your course all that amount more appealing and relatable.

7.4 How to Make Money from Udemy

It's quite simple to attempt to secondary school this. Start with making the right course or layout of the things you wish to cover in your lesson. At the point when done, don't finish it yet. Have another person gone through them, in a perfect world, someone who isn't comfortable alongside your course subject. That approach, you get criticism on whether it's unmistakable, justifiable, or excessively specialized. Somebody who is curious about your course's topic and realizes next to nothing about it can persistently be the ideal analyzer. On the off chance that they have taken in a generous amount from your course and found it intelligible and enlightening, congrats could be a quality one! At that point, construct a video of yourself perusing the full course and have elective individuals read it. Beginning in this manner, you can get target criticism on whether it's reasonable and justifiable.

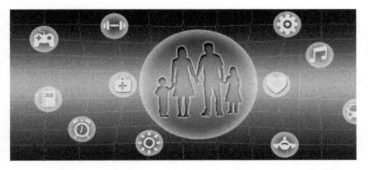

More than basically the course's substance, you may conjointly need to introduce them in an incredible technique that your enrollees can comprehend. They hope to discover from your class and this way. It would help if you gave them their cash's worth. When you get enough reasonable criticism for it, the time has come to shoot the last video for your course. Try not to ration quality here. Put resources into talented sound and video creation if shooting and altering recordings isn't your capacity and spotlight on what you excel at - conveying your course. You would prefer not to wind up completing two things. It's smarter to submit totally to 1 piece of the work and own it to quality, and simply leave the contrary part to an expert. Remember that you can fabricate your seminar available for nothing! This is unquestionably one thing to consider with little opportunity arrives as you start manufacturing your standing. Criticism is close to essential because of the actual pay. The connection between specific criticism and expanded income is not a simple relationship. It is an assurance. In case you're not during a surge and are prepared to require your sweet time to develop this business, at that point, you might need to make your underlying course, or a couple thereof, free.

This way, you limit your danger of building up an unfortunate standing for being somebody who looks for money for inferior quality substance. At now, it's accepted that you as of now have a record with Udemy. If not, feel free to enroll. For a ton of information about it, go straightforwardly to their site and attempt their prerequisites and arrangements. I'm positive you peruse the Terms of Use Agreements at whatever point you set up a record anyplace on the Internet. Anyway, verify you do the indistinguishable here. You are attempting to make money on Udemy. In this way, it assists with being very much aware and educated concerning the site's subtleties. When you have got a record, it's an ideal opportunity to transfer your course. In any case, it doesn't complete there. It is perfect for advancing it outside of Udemy as well. Selling your course at spans the site can be direct for Udemy's situation.

Chapter 8

The Secret of My Money is Affiliate Marketing

In the solitary feasible terms, offshoot showcasing is an uninvolved method for procuring pay basically by advancing elective business visionaries' items or administrations on your web or blog locales. There is a wide range of manners by which of doing subsidiary running anyway regularly talking, you can acquire through commissions - as a level of deals - or attached rates per buy that item or specialist organizations give you at whatever point you peruse click a connection in your web or blog page's substance, are coordinated to the supplier's site and get the item or administration being offered in it. In various subsidiary projects, the guests who were coordinated to them by tapping on connections on your sites don't need to search for only for you to acquire off them - they just need to require bound activities other than getting like selecting in with an email address or finishing an overview, among others. Changes - or real deals - are precisely followed by merchants through a connection given to you (the distributor) that contains a code explicit to you. Sellers use that to work out that of the deals that came from you. Elective sellers may give you a "coupon code" to pass on the way to your peruses, and these coupon codes are the thing that distinguishes explicit deals with you as a distributor. That is the reason for paying your bonuses. Associate showcasing is among the most - if not the most - most popular modes for publicizing by numerous individuals because of expense productivity.

In this chapter, I will walk you through everything you need to know to start affiliate marketing for your passive income.

8.1 Step by Step

•   Picking the correct niche. The most crucial move in the whole process is possible to select your place. A nice niche, such as fashion, beauty, and wellness.

•   Picking the correct forum. You'll need to determine what channel you're going to use to develop your brand and promote affiliate products and services once you've selected your niche (or even before, if you prefer).

•   Enter affiliate programs that are applicable. It is time to join specific affiliate programs now that you know what niche you want to reach and the network you will use.

•   Start to build content and plan your website for it, whether it is a blog, a YouTube channel, email marketing, whatever platform you choose.

•   Drive traffic and subscribers

•   Start promoting your affiliate links

•   Make money with affiliate marketing and blogging

With partner promoting, merchants just acquire publicizing upon change or a particular activity as referenced before. In contrast to conventional publicizing or advancing, merchants don't have to purchase ads that fail to receive any notice or inside the instance of on-line showcasing dazed eyes. This way, the benefit is improved. In different words, associate advancing has considered essential to be rather than conventional implies that of publicizing since it (in some cases) offers one hundred% intensity on the venture. Paying for boards, setting TV adverts, taking an interest in sponsorship programs, and so forth is generally costly and offers no assurance, at all, that deals will increment. In best case scenario, partnerships can utilize educated visualization and consultancy administrations to improve their promoting methods to minimize hazards. For distributors like you, offshoot selling could be a champ simply because it offers the opportunity to find and sell stock that is profoundly pertinent to a particular specialty of decision, which can provide higher pay contrasted with pay-per-click showcasing or standard promoting.

On an angle note, if your blog, any sort of page, or whatever sort of adventure you have going on has amassed an extensive after, it's anything but an extraordinariness to encourage offers from sellers who might potentially wish to promote their product to your crowds. One illustration of such a given I know, from individual experience, is of a supporter who has had a YouTube channel for some time. Some of his instructional exercise recordings on a chose subject accumulated a serious view check, so in some undefined time later on, he was reached by an association whose business was associated with the substance of his recordings. They indeed offered to pay a tight amount of money if he gave them rights to advance their items on said recordings. This methodology he took advantage of his substance for all intents and purposes, and he wasn't in any event, pulling out all the stops! Envision what you'll achieve with a blend of exertion, association, and core interest.

8.2 Things You Didn't Know About Affiliate Marketing

In contrast to specialty sites, the connection between you as a distributor and your peruse is a great deal closer to home or more profound. Such a relationship appreciates a more significant amount of trust and trustworthiness contrasted with an unmistakable fragment site. In that capacity, your blog peruses might be extra disposed to follow your item or administration suggestions when determined with a particular section site. Presently I'm not saying specialty sites suck - I mean, I even included it all together of the approaches to acquire automated revenue. I'm trying to say that for partner advancing elements, publishing content to a blog could get delighted from a higher transformation rate contrasted with specialty market sites. Nonetheless, the tradeoff is that it takes effort for writing for a blog to store up enough steadfast adherents to be beneficial, while specialty selling can give changes bountiful quicker.

Merchants are mindful that the ordinary individual doesn't actually like advertisements, mainly while investing their recreation energy cruising through the Internet. A customer is a ton of a great deal of presumably to test their advert out if it comes from a confided in the stockpile, similar to their #1 blogger. Especially is this the situation if the blogger straightforwardly suggests or supports the product. Presently, with all that trust at the forefront of your thoughts, envision what might happen to your blog on the off chance that you abused that trust to promote an unacceptable item? Goody gumdrops.

8.3 Getting Started with Affiliate Marketing

Indeed, associate showcasing can be worthwhile, but on the other hand, it's not chicken feed. It's not choosing money on trees, as you may have guessed. While a few people do acquire from member selling, just some will procure a fortune since partner selling achievement is very fixated on numerous components, for example, site traffic, item significance, item quality, trust among distributer and peruses, the readiness of peruses to purchase and ability to carefully record extraordinary deals duplicates. What's more, discussing willingness to search for, you may need to utilize alert to ensure that you don't push you peruses to hard or sell inferior quality item since it will not just ruin your probabilities of transforming them to paying clients for your merchants, you moreover may hazard demolishing your entire or individual standing, the last being particularly obvious on the off chance that you are doing partner selling through your blog as opposed to an unmistakable fragment site.

There are bunches of articles on the Internet notice bloggers about the dangers of offshoot promoting, or stories where misinformed publicizing efforts have destroyed fruitful bloggers' professions. Have you continuously followed or withdrawn from a substance maker just because of the assault of adverts, especially awful ones, which irreversibly altered their foundation for the more serious? Haven't you, at any rate, thought of it as now and again? I remember I have, to say the very least! Regardless of how faithful of an after you may have, they'll exclusively be pushed in this manner much before your foundation starts to disintegrate, kind of a place of cards. In this way, practice outrageous alert and always remember your uprightness. Your crowd may often think about it much more than you are doing. Along these lines, how might you truly make money from associate advancing?

Chapter 9

Get Your Hands dirty with Email Marketing

As the name proposes, this can be a method of acquiring automated revenue by utilizing email to offer your item and administrations to people. You wish to have the option to procure automated revenue through email promoting effectively is an email list that could be a rundown of people who bought into your common email dissemination framework, in some cases bulletins, that give them accommodating or eye-catching substance. There are two sorts of email records: conversation and declaration. In conversation records, all the individuals in the rundown approach any of the wide range of various individuals, i.e., sending messages to them. In declaration records, exclusively you as overseer or rundown proprietor can do this.

As a rule, declaration records are fundamentally utilized for sending ordinary email pamphlets and declarations, while conversation records are essential for making virtual networks where individuals who are keen on a particular specialty or subject will examine it together. This collaboration between supporters stretches your conversation email list makes them hidden edges that you'll make keen utilization of. In particular, an interconnected and decentralized local area can consistently share and grow extra adequately. If you wish to make a, Therefore, parcel of the lively local area, this is regularly the way to travel. Declaration email records are more fitting for an all-around grounded local area of supporters, these being standard clients or devotees of your entirety.

In this chapter, I will walk you through everything you need to know to start Email marketing for your passive income.

9.1 How to Build Your Email List

There are two ways to accumulate your list of emails - you develop it or buy it. Taking the time and putting in place the initiative to evaluate your list undoubtedly has quite a few advantages over the alternative for the needs of economic and substantive ads. In more depth, we'll explore both choices. Let's talk about setting it up first.

9.2 Landing Pages: A Powerful Tool for Your Business

The quickest method to construct your email list is by guiding quality traffic to your item or administration's presentation page, and by quality, I mean people who are possibilities, not simple kibitzers or inquisitive felines. One in everything about best places to begin is - shock - Facebook! This can be because promoting on Facebook permits you to zero in on your necessary market, i.e., the legitimate socioeconomics. In unequivocal, you'll pick your commercials' intended interest groups principally dependent on age, sex, area, interests, and even the status of their connections, among others.

This is an indispensable preferred position because the righter or centered you're publicizing is, the extra intense it becomes. Because of the inside and out the detail of individual information that its clients give Facebook, it has since quite a while ago become a site with boundless advancing potential. From more modest to huge ones, numerous organizations see full well of this comfort, that is why they regularly devote sizeable measures of cash to Facebook's promotion programs. On the off chance that I didn't get a handle on any higher, I'd say that this is regularly really one of the first essential elements adding to Facebook's excellent web cost. You can conjointly develop your email list by setting up presentation pages that are explicitly committed to offering uninhibitedly free assets and have hint up structures (where they can leave their email addresses in return for the gifts) that are extremely direct to see.

Furthermore, talking about presentation pages, great ones are the individuals who don't have diverting parts and are focused exclusively on getting people's email addresses in return with the expectation of complimentary assets like reports, eBooks, and diverse downloadable stuff. Numerous destinations work solely for this reason, offering limits, looking through coupons or specialty items, computerized or physical. The simple truth that these locales exist goes to show you exactly how productive this sort of publicizing can be.

9.3 Discount Codes & Vouchers

You can get email delivers to make up your rundown by utilizing a spring up a window that offers your site's guests the chance to ask limits codes in coming for their email addresses. In express, this functions admirably with people who are now acquainted with the items and administrations you are concocting to or are now advancing utilizing email. Even though they are regularly irritating to most, popups can be a great deal of than invited if they make with them those limits or any free stuff. Fundamentally, you'll scarcely miss the point with giveaways. Simply remember that while numerous people pursue the limits, they ordinarily take as much time as necessary in utilizing them. Along these lines, don't get debilitate if this doesn't support your business straight away.

The key here is building connections, which you'll do by reliably giving them free anyway quality substance through email. If your deals are as yet deteriorating when a lot of your time has passed, it would conceivably be an ideal opportunity to change or alter your program in some methodology, especially if you are conveying a massive load of limits and free items. Even though building a veritable relationship alongside your clients is significant, you don't wish to be exploited and fail by giving too a few rebate codes with no real outcome. Discussing markdown codes, you'll effectively fabricate these through an application alluded to as Just Uno, which gives out free plans that you'll use to make an endowment of rebate codes to possibilities in return for their email addresses. Simply make your markdown code, plug it inside the application and tweak how you need it to appear to be on a gadget.

9.4 Buying Email Lists: Reboot Your B2B Lead Generation and Grow Your Business

Looking for email records is entirely lawful and can genuinely make it plentiful, a lot simpler for you because I'll be straightforward - develop an email list needs a huge load of debilitating work, consistency, innovativeness, and time. It's this allure that produces looking for email records so in style nowadays. In this manner, would it be a good idea for you to buy email records and save bountiful exertion and time from speeding things up? No. Nothing. Never. The prominence of this application is unmerited. This is, another model where that old-fashioned saying about clear roads becomes an integral factor - there is no such issue as a direct road. Why? Introductory off, you needn't bother with email addresses for having email addresses. You need acceptable email addresses, i.e., the individuals who are keen possibilities for offering your stuff to. The sole technique your email rundown will be valuable to the promoting in your specific exchange is on the off chance that you constructed it in any case. The lone strategy to guarantee that yours is a quality rundown is if you made it around your particular business.

The interests of individuals on the rundown should relate to that that you're selling. What's more email records that are available to be purchased are not of reasonable quality to the smallest degree. Assume of it this way. On the off chance that you have an excellent rundown of the email tends to that are changing or looking for from you, will you share it to others whether they pay you for it? I question you may - they could even poach your best records from you! Presently does one see why it is reasonable that the lion's share email records are, poo? Another motivation to remain standoffish from purchasing email records is that the people who own those rundowns scarcely remember you if even the slightest bit. If they don't have any acquaintance with you, for what reason would they genuinely think about going to your site?

Further, for what reason should they even choose to keep getting an email from you? They'll simply eliminate themselves from your rundown or divert your messages to the garbage can naturally.

Furthermore, that my companion could be a misuse of cash. Not to say, it will hurt your standing as an email advertiser. More hurt than benefit. Goodness, I'm not done be that as it may. Another motivation to keep away from looking for records at all costs is because of your IP address' (consider it your web advancing id), notoriety will be undermined. Without going into too a few specialized subtleties, sending messages to addresses in an email show, you gained through purchasing runs the opportunity to label and answer the correct enemy of spamming specialists as spam. At the point when this occurs, I would conceivably also bid farewell to your email selling efforts. Keep in mind - spamming is underhanded! Indeed, at least on the planet of web-based promoting, virtually from customers' point of view.

Chapter 10

Creating a Passive Income from a Larger Budget

When putting resources into any cash making undertaking, consistently recollect that everything is relative; the number you can hope to procure is comparative with the danger concerned. A generally safe some of the time implies that there's an espresso loan fee and a high financing cost ordinarily means there's an enormously expanded danger of not exclusively procuring, however of additionally losing your speculation. The best way to check whether one thing will be a beneficial automated revenue stream is by contrasting the reasonable returned and the current danger-free pace of return on, say, government bonds.

Here is the step by step guide to starting passive income from a larger budget to create passive income streams.

10.1 Internet Share Market Investing

Most people have heard how a few people make a tremendous fortune contributing to the financial exchange. In reality, you'll have the option to make considerable cash acquires, putting resources into stocks and offers. There are some basic errors that first-time financial backers need to focus on before they endeavor to put resources into reserves. If you have two or three hundred greenbacks to extra and simply wish to perceive what occurs, that is alright, nonetheless in case you're not kidding for making decent automated revenue; it is a genuine expectation to absorb information like whatever else. Don't just hop in carelessly. However the nuts and bolts of putting are straightforward in principle: buy low and sell high. Most people don't, practically speaking, in any case, catch what high and low very mean. What is high to somebody who is selling is commonly considered low (or sufficiently low) to the purchaser in any exchange. In this manner, various ends can be drawn from similar data. Due to the general idea of the market, it is essential to require an opportunity to examine what stocks or offers are doing before bouncing in.

Before starting, you should gain proficiency with at least the essential measurements, for example, book esteem, partitioned yield, worth profit proportions, and consequently forward.

See how they're determined, where their significant shortcomings lie, and where these measurements have commonly been for any stock and exchange after some time. When you start out, it is beneficial to utilize virtual cash in a stock test system or with a demo account, as this will assist you with seeing how things work and save a significant addition of money in the first place. At the point when you at first examine penny stocks, they appear to be a decent thought. With as next to no as $a hundred, you'll have the option to get significantly a more significant number of offers in penny stocks than you'll if purchasing a blue-chip stock that could cost $50 or extra (some plentiful extra) for a recommendation. Penny stock offers a decent benefit if it goes up by a greenback. Be that as it may, unfortunately, what penny stocks offer in their productivity ought to be estimated against the instability they have. They are alluded to as penny stocks for an explanation; typically, they're lousy quality organizations that, as a rule, won't sort out as a beneficial arrangement. Losing fifty pennies on a penny stock may mean a 100percent misfortune. Losing fifty pennies on a $50 bargain isn't so terrible and will now and then be recovered later, given time. Getting robust data on penny stocks can conjointly be inconvenient, making them a helpless option for a financial backer who remains to learn as they are astoundingly powerless. Generally, it is a decent arrangement to consider stocks in rates and not entire dollar sums.

At the point when you at first start out or work you become experienced in dealing with stocks, most people should claim and oblige quality stock as a drawn-out recommendation instead of endeavoring to make a quick buck on bad quality firms, as most profits for penny stocks involve karma. Try not to be enticed to estimate everything in one explicit venture; usually, it is anything but a decent movie. Any organization, even the least difficult ones, can have issues and see its stocks decrease drastically. This occurred in the last money related accident. Particularly when basically beginning, it is a sound intend to search for exclusively a small bunch of stocks hence you are less without a doubt to possess a colossal misfortune inside the occasion of issues, and generally speaking good and wrong times should level out to call attention to a practical benefit.

The exercises learned while doing this at that point becomes less expensive, yet at the same time necessary. Be appallingly cautious for getting to accept a situation as nothing is ever a positive wagered. On the off chance that you get for stocks, it is alluded to as utilizing your cash. This amplifies both the additions and the misfortunes of given speculation.

10.2 The Common Sense of Earning a Passive Income

It's important to remember that you could, without a doubt, lose every one of your ventures over the evening, so it is indispensable to exclusively utilize the cash you'll have the option to stand to lose. On the off chance that you begin with an underlying venture and construct a couple of gains, take an offer from the benefits and reinvest that. At that point, by gradually increment your all-out speculation, you'll be in a more grounded position while not gambling excessively. Contributing should be seen as a drawn-out business, regardless of whether you are a broker or a looking for and holding sort financial backer.

To remain in business, you might want to have some money on the feature for crises and openings. This money won't acquire any return. Anyway including all your money inside the market might be a danger that even proficient financial backers won't take. On the off chance that you need more money to estimate and save some for crisis cash save, at that point, you are not in a same position monetarily where contributing is keen. Sound guidance is difficult to look out, and to endeavor to figure the accompanying gigantic issue or quickest developing offer worth, hot tips, or working on gossipy tidbits is not a sound field-tested strategy and will be loaded up with perils for introductory time financial backers.

Keep in mind, and you're rivaling proficient companies that not exclusively get information the subsequent it opens up, anyway have had long periods of involvement and perceive how to investigate it rapidly appropriately. In case you're fortunate, you will win a couple, and however, if your karma runs out, you'll lose everything. The least complicated arrangement for fledglings is to remain interested in partnerships you comprehend and have individual experience tending to. You should not deal with contributing like getting a charge out of the lotto. At the point when you are expressly looking for stocks inside the market, you're going up against substantial shared assets and expert financial backers that attempt this full-time and with way different assets and top to bottom data than the essential individual can get. When you first start contributing, it's ideal to begin little and face the challenges with money you are prepared to lose, because the market can be unforgiving to any missteps. As you become a ton of adroit at assessing stocks, you'll begin making more giant speculations.

Chapter 11

Creating a Passive Income from a Small Budget: It's for Everyone

Making an easy revenue on the web could be a fantasy for some people. Anyway it will be a reality for any individual who has a pc and web affiliation. Regardless of whether you're merely starting to incite captivated by chipping away at the net and might want to look out a way to have an easy revenue, or on the off chance that you have been battling to frame a pay from it, there are a couple of things you should ponder before bouncing inside the profound completion of the web pool. You should consider some significant inquiries to assist you with picking your best methodology: Do you have an item or administration you need to sell? This can be an item you have made, whether physical or scholarly. Do you, now, have some sort of essence on the web, a site, blog, or web-based media accounts? Do you have a financial plan? What is your web aptitude? What will you figure out how to be fruitful? There are some fantastic approaches to begin creating an automated revenue while not going through a massive load of cash, notwithstanding even though it is conceivable to maintain a business without spending something, this methodology would, for the most part, be a long cycle and need a goliath amount of work.

The best procedure is to build up spending you'll have the option to manage and work among that. The more principal amount you have in your financial plan, among other reasons, the quicker and more straightforward it's to accomplish a pay level that will uphold your way of life.

Here is the step by step guide to starting passive income from a small budget to create passive income streams.

11.1 Passive Income Streams – Give me Some Ideas Man!

Nonetheless, there are numerous individuals online who work on the rule that it's easy to isolate a simpleton and his cash subsequently be careful! Getting a presence on the web can be cultivated by starting via web-based media locales like Facebook, Google Plus, Twitter, Linked In, YouTube, Pinterest, and Instagram, in addition to utilizing a portion of the lesser-known local online media destinations. The downside with these locales is there, changing into, in this way, jam-packed that the opposition is challenging to adapt to, and it's clear for your undertakings to initiate lost inside the tide of data introduced. A few years back, these destinations functioned admirably. Presently, with over 3.5 Billion people utilizing the net consistently, it takes a touch of skill to use them successfully. Being particular and cautious in where you place your speculation greenbacks is the way to progress.

It's persistently a smart thought to utilize your name on your site. This is because there's no uncertainty about which the situating has a place, and individuals will rapidly relate your name with a top-quality item. That is expecting you essentially have a quality products. If you utilize second rate items and don't offer worth for time and cash spent, you may have an appallingly short future on the web.

If you have an item that you wish to endeavor, yet without your name related to it, you'll utilize one among your sub-areas or produce another one by excluding your name in the web address for that page. For example, you may understand an extraordinary determination of cook's blades and make a plan with the maker or provider to sell them. Hence you'll utilize one among your free subdomains to do this.

• Another decision is you'll want to frame another eBook, for example, a pastry cookbook, and that could be on a sub-space page of your main website, anyway with its independent web presence, connected or unlinked to your primary webpage.

• At the point when you start or be necessary for Bluehost and WordPress or any of the other net facilitating enterprises, they give full bearings on the best way to set up your web site and business, along with a heap of the helpful proposal, subsequently this book can't go into these actual subtleties.

• An uninvolved total compensation might be accomplished by re-appropriating all the compulsory work and just managing the activity, yet that likewise needs some info. Subsequently there's no such factor as a straightforward revenue site.

Having expressed that, it is conceivable, and truly moderate, to have an extremely low upkeep pay webpage, especially if you utilize and get familiar with a portion of the devices and ways accessible from your WordPress site where it is potential to incorporate adaptation into your WordPress site and increment the acquiring capability of your locales with negligible exertion. To shape the chief of those locales, you will, in any case, have to attempt to do all the overall consistent schedule site upkeep assignments like composing new posts, selling, and site support. Anyway the lucrative methodology you are taking can be very straightforward and need little work on your half once set up.

Chapter 12

Rental Property Investment:

Brace Yourself

Investment property venture is arising as a superb opportunity for financial backers as they are on edge about the abrupt droops and piddling additions of the securities exchange. Is it accurate to say that you are going after investment property speculation? Before you set on your journey for an investment property, ensure that you genuinely secure what it likes to be a landowner. Even though it is a productive endeavor, it's anything but a snap using any means. You would need to keep up the property to receive the cash benefits all through your proprietorship time. To a few, investment property speculation is just one thing that includes looking for a house, giving it on a lease, and afterward rounding up greenbacks while unwinding in a very love seat. Be that as it may, this can be a path from being sensible, incredibly if you need an ordinary rental pay for quite a long time to return.

For example, it is smarter to lease a house close by a school since a terrible ton of understudies is conceivable to go searching for a residence inside their staff region. This winds up in an adequate proposal of occupants the entire year-round. In an incredible significance, investment property speculation is all for dissecting the region, doing regardless of it takes to lease your property, keeping your inhabitants cheerful, and keeping up the parcel so it very well may be hired quite a long time after a year in this way limiting the opening period.

In this chapter, I will walk you through everything you need to know to start a rental property investment for your passive income.

12.1 Learn the Benefits of Rental Property Investing

There are numerous advantages to investment property ventures to build your pay over various speculation vehicles. You can, in any case, develop your money by elective methods even with bad economic situations. On account of property being basically justifiable though being ordinary while, it it produces it an entirely practical choice to shape cash. Resources contributing as a profession plausibility can get your business validity and bring in you various of money rapidly because properties that are purchased and sold are genuine and you will continuously have a real decent to bring to the table. Also, somebody can unendingly wish to live on your property. You won't be prepared to sell it for full worth when the market is down, yet you might be ready to sell it. When the market recuperates, you'll have the option to ensure overall goliath revenues from the offer of your properties.

By putting resources into land, one of the favorable circumstances is you settle on the selling estimation of your properties, so it's everything up to you whether you'd go for the low-esteem properties or you'll have the option also to go upscale. With the different properties available, it's dependent upon you to pick which one to broaden your pay. To make your life simpler, you may furthermore have to put resources into the property using a real estate professional, and they'll accomplish all the work. At the same time, you keep on getting your benefit looking like cuts from the deal finished. Putting resources into land might be an amazingly decent chance because of the numerous options available.

The satisfaction you get in realty comes from the cash or benefits you acquire anyway, likewise on the new assets you learn as you arrive. If you need to start putting resources into land, there's no lack of potential wellsprings of information and perusing materials as a ton has just been composed for it. Investment property speculations conjointly make it achievable for you to possess a piece life offset because with this, you're not attached to a regular eight-5, and you just work when you might want to. How you lead your speculations is totally up to you. This speculation also offers the comfort of being observed and overseen directly in your home office. A lot of it is directing calls, investigating and meeting with benefactors and vendors, so you will be prepared to figure from anyplace in the region. Obviously, as in any business, you may contribute because you wish the money benefits. For each effective deal, a financial backer is ensured of gigantic measures of money. There could be hazards because of the way that vast amounts of money are included. It will be a terrifying idea to lose a great deal around here, yet in the tip, everything levels out with the tremendous measures of money to be procured as a genuine domain financial backer making it an advantageous undertaking any way you investigate it. Investment property speculations satisfy its guarantee of remunerations not just monetarily anyway additionally the advantage of brain and comfort by having the option to figure from home at your own time. However long you hold doing it, and with the appropriate apparatuses, technique, and information, you might be reimbursed in manners by which you have never envisioned.

12.2 A Short Guide on Rental Property Investment

Thus, you have this cash inside the bank, and one of the ideas you're playing with is investment property speculation. Notwithstanding, you don't know what essential things to search for or ask your resources representative as route as picking a good piece of property is concerned. Try not to worry because here might be a wise fundamental guide you'll examine with first off: Your investment property speculation should be in a sensitive area. A quality area is one of all the components of productive property. Forthcoming occupants are perpetually pursuing places that will cause them to feel they have a home. For instance, if your property is closed to Information Technology focuses, conceivable outcomes are your eventual inhabitants work in that exchange. Another model: your property may be situated in an expanding local area with a massive load of youthful families, so anticipate that your home or loft should speak to couples with next to no young people.

Along these lines, select property in an incredible neighborhood with a shrewd security annual and an exceptionally responsive police power. Get some information about the historical backdrop of the spot to offer you a decent image of security levels that your future inhabitants can doubtlessly request to look out the. Your investment property venture ought to be closed to work openings. In this economic environment, people can continuously be the place where the jobs are, so to make positive your speculation transforms into productive land, select a spot near those chances. For instance: a genuine company is gapping a satellite working environment in your town, or maybe moving its base camp. That is your likelihood to cash in on the people who might want a territory near that foundation. Fabricate accommodation your offering reason to intrigued occupants! Choosing an area to put resources into and get easy revenue from ought not to be confounded. However long you factor in the higher than parts in your call-production, you'll relish the advantages and awards of your investment property very much into your retirement.

Before you purchase your first investment property, put your business substance together, gapping with a strong business set up. Your field-tested strategy should cover. Personally each progression in the securing of a property, from the elevating strategy to search out the correct occupants, rent choice, and rental term arrangements and proceed through the offer of the property. Visit your neighborhood realty financial backers' affiliation.

12.3 Rental Property Investment Analysis - The Essential Guide to doing it correctly!

Generally, medium to massive networks have a property contributing club where such a realty financial backer returns together at much of the time planned gatherings. Take masses of business cards and gather them moreover. Your prosperity will exist in the associations you make and keep up all through the entire time you are a landowner with investment properties. A few key variables are thought of, mainly if this is regularly drawn-out speculation. The correct real estate professional won't exclusively encourage you to locate the best property. He will likewise encourage supplant inhabitants after some time, so it could be a lifetime asset that you may wish to associate with and feel guaranteed alongside his experience.

Understand a genuine home specialist that comprehends financial property backers. The objectives of investment property contributing are not the same as those of an ordinary home purchaser. The pay and costs of investment property contributing will shift after some time. A few months, you'll bring in cash, and a few months, you will make back the initial investment or have a few costs to cover up. Later on, the significant domain market has persistently been the best venture. On the off chance that you have a business set up that factors in the good and bad times, you should be productive after some time. A specialist who comprehends investment property contributing can also explore reasonable arrangements and the appropriate area.

Opening doesn't create any pay. They additionally value your cash. Before you put resources into any investment property, you should shield yourself by examining the rental market. Check the recurrence of rental postings in your neighborhood paper and address all or any of the real estate professionals and property chiefs in the domain that you can. Investment properties in certain areas close to resources or colleges have a preferred interest for rentals over others. When you own an investment property, you are ready to go. You are not just a financial backer. To maintain your business effectively, you need to submit enough some time and assets that are essential. It is fundamental that you practically see how much cash and time you may pay before you make an interest in an investment property. Whether you're effectively concerned day by day, you recruit a chief to maintain the business for you.

CONCLUSION

Much obliged to you for purchasing this book. Presently that you've figured out how to procure automated revenue through the Net, you're prepared to expand your pay while not crushing your spirit - or the bank. Notwithstanding, knowing is essentially the fight. The inverse is applying what you realized. I exceptionally urge you to utilize what you've learned here or become familiar with extra in regards to the frameworks I have printed. One way or the other, you'll be following up on what you have realized. By sitting idle, you are simply left with an engaging book and, generally, random data. Activity is the situation here. Even though it might happen on more than one occasion in a too lifetime, you proceed to can't rely on useful things returning unexpectedly.

Moreover, it's smarter to spend "a few times" stipend on more challenging things in life than work, much the same as the feared connections! The thing least conceivable to return all alone is the opportunity, autonomy. This has gotten unquestionably valid for the globe we possess these days. For what reason would I say that? Indeed, I say it because they don't want you to be free and work for yourself. This isn't some paranoid fear possibly; it is somewhat the personality of the monster called Economy. Presently, I'm not saying that "work" or "occupations" are an undesirable factor. I'm positive that there are many people who are extra than pleased with their ordinary line of work. Nor am I advancing lethargy, so much from it, God deny! If you have taken in anything from this book, it's that easy revenue, notwithstanding its name, will require assurance, exertion, and time - work!

Nonetheless, the secret to the present here business, or rather the entire motivation behind it, is to put that work into an issue. It is building this framework with its point working for you. In any business, someone needs to figure for it to run and be productive. Anyway here, it's concerning causing the innovation to be that "someone." It's for bridging the boundless capability of the Web, which we will, in general, take completely as a correct these days.

It's a wrongdoing against us, against our latent capacity, to substantial innovative headway aside as something that impedes our vocation, something that is out to ask us. The people who spout such cases and maxims are either too reluctant even to consider requiring those initial steps or are malignant and don't need you to succeed. Since let me advise you, the sole thing that innovation incredibly compromises is our shackles and others' adaptability to control our fate. Pay no brain to doubters. Do take a proposal where realistic and learn, learn, learn, however, don't leave yourself alone debilitate by individuals who exclusively need to hamper progress because of 25 their frailties. Fortunately, those aren't strenuous to spot! You will tell a pessimist without reason effectively by attempting where they stand or a great deal of precisely deteriorating. Online automated revenue is genuine. Well it's been real for quite a while; notwithstanding, it is a great deal of unmistakable at present than at any other time. Accordingly, make the accompanying stride towards effectively procuring automated revenue! May the chances be ever in support of you! Recall that fortune will support the bold! Cheers!

About the author Rebecca Rightime

Rebecca is a young 35 year old career woman working in the field of finance and investment in the in-house PR department. She lives in London and really enjoys her city because she has the opportunity to talk to people from different cultures and find out lots of interesting information. She loves going to pubs but she also often goes to bookstores during her free time. She is married to James and has recently had twins who take up most of her time, but with good organization and the help of new technologies she still manages to do everything. She also has a very lively cat named Tom who often makes her angry because he jumps everywhere and knocks over her vases and furniture. Rebecca is curious, she has a good gab; in fact when you meet her she doesn't stop talking and asking questions. She is a very sociable and dynamic person. In her free time she loves to go trekking with her friends and she is also a member of some local sport associations, she likes travelling, the sea and the cheesecakes she learned to make from her maternal grandmother.

CPSIA information can be obtained
at www.ICGtesting.com
Printed in the USA
BVHW041515190321
602997BV00010B/542

9 781802 221435